STUDY GUIDE

Inventing America

A History of the United States

Volume 2

Inventing America

A History of the United States

VOLUME 2

Pauline Maier • Merritt Roe Smith
Alexander Keyssar • Daniel J. Kevles

Wendy Wall

COLGATE UNIVERSITY

 W • W • NORTON & COMPANY • NEW YORK • LONDON

ISBN 0-393-97828-1 (pbk.)

W. W. Norton & Company, Inc., 500 Fifth Avenue, New York, N.Y. 10110
www.wwnorton.com

W. W. Norton & Company Ltd., Castle House, 75/76 Wells Street, London W1T 3QT

1 2 3 4 5 6 7 8 9 0

CONTENTS

PREFACE

In its ability to survey the broad expanse of American history from the perspective of innovation, *Inventing America: A History of the United States* is unique. The Study Guide is specially designed to complement and enhance this remarkable textbook. Its nine supplementary tools help students get the most out of each chapter by preparing them for their reading and testing their comprehension of the material presented. It also facilitates further exploration of history by guiding them to additional readings, videos, and online resources.

There is no prescribed way to use the Study Guide to *Inventing America*, but the study aids are presented in roughly chronological sequence, following a three-stage process. First, students will want to read the "Chapter Objectives," scan the "Chapter Outline," and review the "Chronology" before reading the corresponding chapter in the text. These aids provide a preview of the events, ideas, and developments discussed in each chapter and will help students situate the chapter within both the text and the entire span of American history. Second, after reading each chapter, students should answer the essay questions, the multiple-choice questions, and the true-or-false questions to test their comprehension and identify areas of weakness that can be bolstered with further review. Third, the Sources for Further Research, including books, videos, and Web resources, will help students extend their learning experience beyond the text. These sources can be used to pursue advanced research and writing projects and will lend a visual and interactive dimension to students' understanding of American history.

Individual students and instructors will find different ways to use the study aids and are encouraged to experiment and innovate. For example, some of the aids lend themselves to group work among students, both inside and outside the classroom. Others may be used to structure in-class discussions, support oral or visual presentations, or encourage online interactions. Each of the nine study aids exhibits some basic features that should guide its use:

- The chapter objectives provide a preview of the six to ten major topics examined in each chapter of *Inventing America* to help students structure their reading. By asking students to summarize or discuss the chapter's main points, they provide a set of goals to keep in mind and promote a more focused reading and learning experience.
- Chapter outlines situate factual details and fundamental ideas within the broad sweep of each chapter. Students can use these outlines, which go beyond the textbook's headings and subheadings, to prepare for their reading and to review basic concepts and facts after completing each chapter.
- The chronology helps students relate diverse episodes and grounds each chapter in the broad narrative of American history. Overall, students can glean a sense of the pace of change across history, as well as the simultaneity of otherwise disparate events, by studying each chronology.
- A set of five or more essay questions highlight major themes developed within each chapter. Questions might ask students to compare and contrast, chart a sequence of events, break down large concepts into their component parts, or resolve apparent contradictions. In some cases, they require students to draw on facts and ideas presented in more than one chapter.
- The multiple-choice and true-or-false questions permit students to review each chapter and to test their understanding of the reading.
- The "Books" section of "Sources for Further Research" includes a sampling of the most important books students can consult to extend their understanding of history. These short bibliographies are meant to point students toward accessible, engaging, and fruitful sources rather than to exhaust the possibilities for study.
- The "Videos" section offers a sampling of the best videos on topics covered in each chapter to be viewed by students as a group or individually. Most originated as television documentaries; some represent big-screen treatments of historical subjects. The documentaries listed are more abundant for later periods of history: the invention of photography in the 1840s and motion pictures in the 1890s stimulated the production of historical images on a wide scale.
- The final study aid is, fittingly, the most technologically advanced: the Web resources. Most of the resources listed originated from museum exhibits, historic sites, academic programs, government agencies, and television productions. Students, however, should note that websites are rarely subject to peer review or supported by footnotes, and they can contain factual flaws and interpretive shortcomings. In general, they are best exploited as visual supplements rather than as definitive texts. Further, websites are by nature transitory, and students may find the addresses presented here already out-of-date. The recommended websites therefore represent a starting point for an exploration of Internet resources rather than a definitive list.

Students will find *Inventing America* a rewarding, provocative, and innovative textbook, and the Study Guide will enhance their experience of reading and learning from its panoramic view of American history. The Study Guide offers a wide range of resources to help students preview text chapters; follow the ideas, facts, and chronologies they encounter within; review the reading and prepare for examinations; and, finally, extend and continue their historical experience well beyond both the text and the classroom.

Wendy Wall
Kenneth J. Winkle

CHAPTER 17 | Reconstruction: 1865–1877

CHAPTER OBJECTIVES

- Discuss the impact of the Civil War on the North, South, and West. Describe the issues that were settled by the war and the issues that still needed to be addressed.
- Compare and contrast the plans for Reconstruction put forward by Abraham Lincoln, Andrew Johnson, and the Radical Republicans in Congress, including specific provisions of each.
- Explain the growing conflict between Andrew Johnson and Congress, including the reasons for Johnson's impeachment.
- Discuss the course of Reconstruction in the southern states, including its effects on former slaves and white southerners.
- Describe the developments in both the North and South that ultimately led to the abandonment of Reconstruction.
- Assess the overall impact of Reconstruction on African Americans, the South, and the nation as a whole.

CHAPTER OUTLINE

I.   The Nation After the Civil War
   A.   Critical Issues Settled by the North's Victory
      1)   Southern states would not secede
      2)   Slavery would be abolished
   B.   Lingering Questions
      1)   Readmission of the Confederate states to the Union
      2)   Treatment of ex-Confederate leaders
      3)   Fate of former slaves
   C.   The Rest of the Nation

1

       1) Rise of industry and manufacturing to political and economic prominence

       2) Opening of the trans-Mississippi West

II. The Fate of the Union

    A. Reconstruction in Wartime

       1) The slavery question

          a) Emancipation Proclamation

          b) Thirteenth Amendment

       2) Reconstituting the Union

          a) Lincoln's Ten-Percent Plan

          b) Wade-Davis Bill

       3) Aid for freed slaves

          a) efforts at land confiscation

          b) federal experiments in land and labor policy

          c) creation of the Freedmen's Bureau

    B. Andrew Johnson and Presidential Reconstruction

       1) Johnson's background and political beliefs

       2) Johnson's plan for Reconstruction

          a) amnesty for former Confederates

          b) restitution of property, except slaves

          c) state governments

       3) The white South's defiance

          a) ex-Confederates elected

          b) Black Codes

       4) Congressional Republicans' response

          a) expanding and extending the Freedmen's Bureau

          b) Civil Rights Bill

          c) Congress vs. Johnson

    C. The Fourteenth Amendment

       1) Provisions

          a) defines citizenship and its rights

          b) enshrines principle of "equality before law"

       2) Impact on 1866 midterm elections

    D. Radical Reconstruction and the Impeachment of Andrew Johnson

       1) Congressional Radicals' Reconstruction plan

          a) reinstituted military authority, except in Tennessee

          b) required states to ratify Fourteenth Amendment

          c) embraced black suffrage

       2) Tenure of Office Act

       3) Impeachment of Andrew Johnson

          a) reasons

          b) trial and acquittal

    E. The Defeat of Land Reform

       1) Reasoning of supporters

2) Conflict with basic Republican values
3) Rejection of Stevens's plan
4) Southern states readmitted to union
  F. The Election of 1868
1) Nomination and election of Ulysses Grant
2) Fifteenth Amendment
III. The Recovering South
  A. A Land Shattered by War
1) Physical devastation
2) Economic collapse
  B. The Experience of Freedom
1) Ex-slaves' reactions to emancipation
    a) moving
    b) family reunification
    c) churches
    d) schools
    e) challenging deference and segregation
2) Southern whites' reactions to emancipation
    a) fear of social equality
    b) race riots and the Ku Klux Klan
  C. Land and Labor
1) Conflicting needs and desires of freedmen and southern whites
2) The emergence of sharecropping
3) The crop-lien system
4) Stagnation of the southern economy
IV. The Road to Redemption
  A. Economic Boom in the North and West
  B. The Republican Party in the South
1) Black voters and officeholders
2) Reconstruction state governments
  C. The Grant Administration
1) Civil service reform
2) Governmental corruption
3) The Enforcement Acts
  D. The Election of 1872
1) Liberal Republican Party
2) Grant's victory
  E. Reconstruction in Retreat
1) Redeemers score political victories
2) Panic of 1873
3) Supreme Court restricts interpretation of Fourteenth and Fifteenth Amendments
  F. The Election of 1876 and the Compromise of 1877
1) Disputed returns

2) Federal troops withdrawn from South
V. Legacies
   A. The Fate of Freed Slaves
   B. Economic Legacies
   C. Political Legacies

CHRONOLOGY

1863	Abraham Lincoln issues the Emancipation Proclamation. Lincoln announces his Ten-Percent Plan for Reconstruction.
1864	Arkansas, Tennessee, and Louisiana establish governments.
1865	Freedmen's Bureau created. Thirteenth Amendment ratified. Lincoln's assassination. Andrew Johnson launches presidential Reconstruction.
1865–66	Southern states institute Black Codes.
1866	Congress passes Civil Rights Bill over Johnson's veto. Ku Klux Klan founded. Congress approves the Fourteenth Amendment. Tennessee readmitted to Congress. Republicans sweep midterm congressional elections.
1867	Congressional Reconstruction begins with the Military Reconstruction Act. Congress passes Tenure of Office Act. Thaddeus Stevens's land reform proposal defeated.
1867–68	Southern states hold constitutional conventions.
1868	Fourteenth Amendment ratified. House impeaches President Johnson; Senate acquits him. Seven more southern states readmitted to Congress. Ulysses S. Grant elected president.
1869	Congress approves the Fifteenth Amendment. Transcontinental railroad completed. Democratic Redeemers begin to win power in the South.
1870	Fifteenth Amendment ratified. Last three southern states readmitted to Congress.
1870–71	Congress passes the Enforcement Acts.
1872	Credit Mobilier scandal exposed.
1873	Panic of 1873 launches economic depression. Supreme Court decides *Slaughterhouse Cases*.

1874	Democrats win control of House for first time since 1856.
1875	Civil Rights Act passed.
	Mississippi Redeemers institute the "Mississippi Plan."
1876	Disputed Hayes-Tilden presidential election produces political crisis.
1877	Compromise of 1877 leads to inauguration of Rutherford B. Hayes.
	President Hayes withdraws all federal troops from the South.
	Last remaining Republican governments in the South fall.

ESSAY QUESTIONS

1. What sectional and racial questions did the Civil War resolve, and what questions remained to be answered in the postwar period?

2. How and why did the plans for Reconstruction put forward by Abraham Lincoln, Andrew Johnson, and the congressional Republicans differ? Do you see any similarities between the plans?

3. What problems did African Americans in the South face after emancipation? How did the government attempt to solve these problems, and what did blacks themselves do? How did everyday life change for the former slaves? (Consider the impact of freedom and Reconstruction on families, community institutions like churches and schools, and labor systems in the South.)

4. How was the contested election of 1876 decided? What were the political, racial, and sectional effects of that decision?

5. Evaluate the impact of Reconstruction. What were its major achievements and failures? Consider both the federal program of Reconstruction (presidential and congressional) and the programs of Radical state governments in the South. Be as specific as possible.

OBJECTIVE QUESTIONS

Multiple Choice

1. Slavery was abolished throughout the nation by:
   a) the Emancipation Proclamation
   b) the Thirteenth Amendment
   c) the Fourteenth Amendment
   d) the Civil Rights Bill of 1866

2. Both Abraham Lincoln and Andrew Johnson believed that Reconstruction:

a) should punish the South
b) could not heal the rifts between North and South
c) should include mass land redistribution to former slaves
d) was primarily the responsibility of the executive branch

3. Andrew Johnson, who became president after Lincoln's assassination, was:
   a) a Democrat from Tennessee
   b) a vociferous supporter of the Union
   c) a former slaveholder
   d) all of the above

4. The Black Codes of 1865 and 1866 were:
   a) part of Andrew Johnson's plan for presidential Reconstruction
   b) proposed by Radical Republicans in Congress to give equal rights to former slaves
   c) passed by southern state governments to restrict the civil, social, and economic behavior of the freedmen
   d) codes of conduct established by the newly formed Ku Klux Klan

5. The Fourteenth Amendment:
   a) guaranteed all persons "the equal protection of the laws"
   b) reaffirmed the Supreme Court's 1857 *Dred Scott* decision
   c) gave all men and women the right to vote, regardless of race
   d) automatically readmitted all southern states to the Union

6. Johnson was impeached for allegedly violating the:
   a) Wade-Davis Bill
   b) Civil Rights Act of 1866
   c) Fourteenth Amendment
   d) Tenure of Office Act

7. A plan to confiscate Confederate lands and redistribute them to the freedmen:
   a) was advocated by Radical Republicans, most notably Congressman Thaddeus Stevens of Pennsylvania and Senator Charles Sumner of Massachusetts
   b) conflicted with basic Republican values
   c) died in Congress in 1867
   d) all of the above

8. African Americans responded to emancipation in all of the following ways except:
   a) moving away from the places where they had been enslaved
   b) rioting against their former masters
   c) marrying and taking last names
   d) building churches and schools

9. The crop-lien system that emerged in the South after the Civil War:
   a) appeared to offer advantages to both farmers and merchants
   b) often trapped small farmers in a system of "debt peonage"
   c) made the South's economy excessively dependent on cotton
   d) all of the above

10. In the late 1860s and early 1870s, Republican governments in southern states:
    a) passed laws instituting segregation in public facilities
    b) sought to encourage railroad construction and industrial growth
    c) cracked down on bribery and other forms of public corruption
    d) all of the above

11. Supporters of the Republican Party in the South included all of the following except:
    a) upcountry whites
    b) African Americans
    c) Redeemers
    d) migrants from the North

12. Tammany Hall was:
    a) the Tennessee convention hall where the Ku Klux Klan held their annual convocations
    b) a New York City political machine run by Democratic boss William Marcy Tweed
    c) a Georgia church established by former slaves
    d) none of the above

13. The Enforcement Acts:
    a) were passed by Congress in 1870 and 1871 in response to an escalation of violence in the South
    b) enlarged federal power
    c) temporarily crippled the Ku Klux Klan
    d) all of the above

14. Redeemers supported:
    a) the restoration of "home rule" to the South
    b) the use of state funds for internal improvements
    c) a repeal of lien laws that gave landlords the first claim on crops
    d) all of the above

15. All of the following contributed to the end of Reconstruction except:
    a) the Panic of 1873
    b) the Credit Mobilier scandal
    c) the Supreme Court decision in the *Slaughterhouse Cases*
    d) the Compromise of 1877

True or False

1. Congress established the Freedmen's Bureau in 1865 to monitor the condition of ex-slaves and to deliver fuel, food, and clothing to the destitute.

2. Andrew Johnson's plan for Reconstruction allowed African Americans who had fought for the Union to vote.

3. Radical Republicans in Congress were outnumbered from the start by the moderates and conservatives in their party.

4. President Johnson was impeached and removed from office in 1868.

5. The Fifteenth Amendment affected only the South, since African Americans in all northern states were already guaranteed the right to vote.

6. In tobacco- and cotton-growing regions of the South, patterns of land ownership, wealth, and power changed substantially in the wake of the Civil War.

7. Southern whites often responded to what they saw as black "impudence" or "disrespect" by taking the law into their own hands. In numerous southern cities, white mobs attacked African Americans during Reconstruction.

8. By 1880, nearly half of all rural southern blacks owned land.

9. The system of sharecropping that emerged in the South after the Civil War allowed blacks to work in family units and gave them a measure of autonomy and independence.

10. During Reconstruction, large numbers of African Americans participated in electoral politics for the first time in the nation's history.

11. By energetically battling the "spoils system" and other forms of corruption and cronyism, the Grant administration helped restore the power and prestige of the presidency.

12. In 1872, both the Liberal Republican and Democratic Parties nominated the journalist Horace Greeley for president.

13. The "Mississippi Plan" was the Grant administration's plan for combating racial violence in the South.

14. The income gap between the North and South that opened during and after the Civil War did not start to narrow until after World War II.

15. The wording of the Fourteenth and Fifteenth Amendments opened the door to women's greater participation in electoral politics in the late nineteenth century.

SOURCES FOR FURTHER RESEARCH

Books

Michael Les Benedict, *The Impeachment and Trial of Andrew Johnson* (1973)
Ira Berlin et al., eds., *Freedom: A Documentary History*, 3 vols. (1985–91)
Laura F. Edwards, *Gendered Strife and Confusion: The Political Culture of Reconstruction* (1997)
Eric Foner, *Reconstruction: America's Unfinished Revolution, 1863–1877* (1988)
Herbert G. Gutman, *The Black Family in Slavery and Freedom* (1976)
Jacqueline Jones, *Labor of Love, Labor of Sorrow* (1985)
Leon Litwack, *Been in the Storm Too Long: The Aftermath of Slavery* (1979)
Nell Irvin Painter, *Exodusters* (1977)
Howard N. Rabinowitz, *Race Relations in the Urban South, 1865–1890* (1978)
Edward Royce, *The Origins of Southern Sharecropping* (1993)

Videos

Abolition: Broken Promises (50 minutes, Films for the Humanities and Sciences, 1998). This program presents a grim picture of the black experience after slavery through the eyes of those who experienced it and their progeny.

Dr. Toer's Amazing Magic Lantern Show (24 minutes, American Social History Project). At the end of the Civil War, a freed slave and Baptist minister named J. W. Toer traveled the South holding public meetings of men and women recently freed from slavery. Historical documents show that these meetings featured a "magic lantern show" entitled "The Progress of Reconstruction" that illustrated the enormous changes then taking place in the South. The video, complete with Dr. Toer's touring company, helps us imagine what Dr. Toer's show might have been like and provides a unique look at the Civil War and Reconstruction from the point of view of the freed slaves.

Found Voices: The Slave Narratives (22 minutes, Films for Humanities and Sciences, 1999). In this program, Ted Koppel of ABC News uses digitally remastered tapes made during the 1930s and 1940s to present the African American slave experience in the voices of those who knew it firsthand. Ex-slaves, including 101-year-old Fountain Hughes, born in 1848, give their recollections of life before emancipation and during Reconstruction.

Web Resources

The Library of Congress's on-line exhibition "The African American Odyssey: A Quest for Full Citizenship" showcases materials from the library's incomparable

African American collections, including material on freed slaves' experiences during Reconstruction.

http://memory.loc.gov/ammem/aaohtml/exhibit/aointro.html

The "Freedmen's Bureau Online" contains marriage and other documents generated by the Freedmen's Bureau as well as links to other related sites.

http://www.freedmensbureau.com

Excerpts from slave narratives, including some dealing with the experience of emancipation and Reconstruction, can be found at

http://vi.uh.edu/pages/mintz/primary.htm

CHAPTER 18 | The Rise of Big Business and the Triumph of Industry: 1870–1900

CHAPTER OBJECTIVES

- Describe the reasons for the rapid industrialization that followed the Civil War.
- Account for the rise of "big business" in the late nineteenth century, and describe the new managerial techniques and business practices it ushered in.
- Discuss the South and the West as "peripheries," comparing and contrasting their regional cultures.
- Describe the factors fueling immigration after the Civil War, and outline the similarities and differences between the "new" and "old" immigrants.

CHAPTER OUTLINE

I. The United States in 1876
   A. Centennial Exhibition Celebrates Progress and Technology
   B. Economic Depression and Social Strife
II. An Industrial Economy
   A. Agriculture and Industry
      1) Agricultural expansion
         a) production spurt
         b) new technologies
         c) falling prices
      2) Industrial expansion
         a) leading industries: machinery, iron, and steel
         b) reasons
         c) emergence of business cycles
   B. Railroads
      1) Wave of railroad construction

    2) New techology and managerial methods
    3) Economic and cultural impact
    4) Public regulation
    5) Railroad mergers
  C. Big Business
    1) The rise of big business
    2) Structural characteristics of big business
      a) distinct operating units
      b) hierarchical management with salaried executives
    3) Changes in business practice
      a) mass distribution
      b) mass production
    4) Paths to bigness
      a) vertical and horizontal integration
      b) pools, trusts, holding companies, and mergers
    5) Regulation
      a) by the states
      b) Sherman Anti-Trust Act
  D. Industry and Technology
    1) Emergence of science-based industries
    2) New technological systems
      a) railroads
      b) telegraph
      c) telephone
      d) electricity
    3) Sources of technological advance
      a) European scientists
      b) independent inventors
      c) corporate research labs
III. The Center and the Periphery
  A. The South
    1) Dependence on agriculture, particularly cotton
    2) Persistent poverty
  B. The West
    1) The peopling of the trans-Mississippi West
      a) sources of migration
      b) desire to settle and farm
      c) challenge of farming: aridity
    2) Trend away from consolidation
      a) farming
      b) cattle ranching
    3) Extractive industries tied to global markets and outside capital
IV. Classes
  A. Changes in Class Structure

      1) Emergence of a national elite
      2) Rise of the new middle class
      3) Huge and growing working class
  B. Jobs and Incomes
      1) Divisions within the working class
         a) skilled, semiskilled, and unskilled
         b) men vs. women
      2) Workplace hazards
         a) physical dangers and disease
         b) job insecurity
      3) Impact of workplace technology
  C. Immigrants and Migrants
      1) Scope of immigration
      2) Sources: "new" vs. "old" immigrants
      3) Global phenomenon
      4) Immigrants a significant proportion of the working class
  D. Social Mobility
      1) The ideology
      2) The reality

CHRONOLOGY

1862	Homestead Act makes free land available. Morrill Act authorizes "land-grant" colleges.
1866	Texas cattle drives begin.
1868–74	Midwestern states pass "Granger" laws to regulate railroads.
1869	Transcontinental railroad completed.
1870	John D. Rockefeller incorporates Standard Oil Company of Ohio.
1872	Thomas Edison invents the stock ticker.
1873	Panic of 1873 ushers in five-year depression. Supreme Court decides *Slaughterhouse Cases*.
1876	Centennial Exhibition in Philadelphia. Alexander Graham Bell patents the telephone.
1877	Supreme Court decides *Munn v. Illinois*.
1879	Edison invents the incandescent lightbulb.
1882	Economic downturn begins and lasts three years. Edison's electric company lights Wall Street. Rockefeller's Standard Oil Company becomes the nation's first trust. Nineteenth-century immigration to the United States peaks.

1883	Railroads divide the United States into standard time zones.
1885	Supreme Court decides *Wabash v. Illinois.*
1886–87	Severe winter and drought cycle in the West cause collapse of cattle boom.
1887	Passage of the Interstate Commerce Act. Hatch Act establishes agricultural experiment stations.
1889	New Jersey passes law legalizing holding companies.
1890	Congress passes the Sherman Anti-Trust Act. Superintendent of the census announces the closing of the frontier.
1893	Stock market panic precipitates severe depression, lasting until 1897.
1900	General Electric founds the first formal research lab in American industry.
1901	U.S. Steel becomes the nation's first billion-dollar corporation.
1903	Orville and Wilbur Wright fly the first airplane.

ESSAY QUESTIONS

1. What accounts for the rise of big business in the United States after the Civil War? What were the consequences of this consolidation? Why didn't agricultural enterprises in the West experience the same kind of consolidation seen among eastern enterprises?

2. An eminent historian once suggested that the economic history of the United States in the late nineteenth century could be told through the history of the railroads. How did railroads stimulate the economy, both regional and national, in this period and what business practices did they pioneer?

3. Compare and contrast the entrepreneurial strategies of James B. Duke, John D. Rockefeller, and the founder of Montgomery Ward.

4. What role did technology play in stimulating the economic boom that followed the Civil War? What impact did new technologies and forms of production have on American workers?

5. In what sense were the "new" immigrants of the late nineteenth and early twentieth centuries new? How did their story intersect with the story of America's rapid industrialization during the same period?

OBJECTIVE QUESTIONS

Multiple Choice

1. Manufacturing output began to exceed agricultural output in the United States:
   a) in the 1840s
   b) in the 1860s
   c) in the 1880s
   d) in 1900

2. The United States' postwar economic expansion was fueled by:
   a) population growth
   b) the expansion of the railroads
   c) the steel industry
   d) all of the above

3. During the economic boom of the late nineteenth century, America's manufacturing center moved:
   a) north
   b) south
   c) east
   d) west

4. The first transcontinental railroad was completed in:
   a) 1865
   b) 1869
   c) 1875
   d) 1883

5. All of the following made fortunes in railroads except:
   a) Leland Stanford
   b) Cornelius Vanderbilt
   c) Jay Gould
   d) Andrew Carnegie

6. The inventor of the refrigerated freight car was:
   a) George Corliss
   b) George Westinghouse
   c) Gustavus Swift
   d) James Bonsack

7. Hierarchical management techniques were pioneered in the United States by:
   a) the steel industry
   b) railroad corporations
   c) the meatpacking industry
   d) the banking industry

8. The explosion in railroad construction in the late nineteenth century benefited:
   a) Chicago
   b) Sears, Roebuck
   c) the steel industry
   d) all of the above

9. The rise of big business in the late nineteenth century:
   a) was linked to the rise of mass distribution and mass production
   b) prompted Congress to pass the Sherman Anti-Trust Act in 1890
   c) resulted in the disappearance of the more than 1,800 independent firms between 1895 and 1904
   d) all of the above

10. The telegraph has been called the "Victorian Internet" because it:
    a) changed the structure of communications after the Civil War, making rapid communication possible throughout the United States and across the Atlantic
    b) prompted an economic boom as thousands of small entrepreneurs rushed to take advantage of the new technology
    c) allowed the senders of messages to disguise their identity
    d) all of the above

11. Industrial research labs:
    a) went hand in hand with the rise of large corporations
    b) allowed companies to select their own research problems, control patents, and thus perpetuate their own market supremacy
    c) provided jobs for those in the emerging profession of engineering
    d) all of the above

12. The South's persistent poverty in the decades following the Civil War can be attributed to all of the following except:
    a) the region's dependence on a single crop, cotton
    b) the abundance of cheap labor
    c) an oppressive system of taxation
    d) northern ownership of many railroads and manufacturing plants in the South

13. The superintendent of the census announced that the frontier line had disappeared in:
    a) 1870
    b) 1880
    c) 1890
    d) 1900

14. All of the following led to the demise of huge cattle ranches by the late 1880s except:

a) Indian attacks
b) severe winter and summer weather
c) overgrazing
d) the disappearance of investors

15. The United States's rapid industrialization in the late nineteenth century produced:
    a) a rise in the proportion of skilled workers in the labor force
    b) better working conditions for most laborers
    c) the emergence of "unemployment"
    d) all of the above

True or False

1. Improved transportation and the resulting internationalization of markets contributed to the decline in the prices of U.S. farm products in the late nineteenth century.

2. The South's cotton crop grew enormously between 1865 and 1900, largely because of improvements in farm machinery.

3. The massive wave of railroad construction between 1865 and 1900 was financed almost entirely by private investors.

4. "Granger" laws represented one of the first efforts by public authorities in the United States to regulate the behavior of private corporations.

5. Henry Ford introduced the techniques of mass production in the 1920s.

6. "Vertical integration" is the process by which a firm controls the entire production process from raw materials to the consumer.

7. In 1889, New York became the first state to pass laws legalizing holding companies.

8. The first "invention factory" was established in Menlo Park, New Jersey, by Alexander Graham Bell.

9. Advocates of a "New South" sought to promote railroads and manufacturing and to reduce the region's dependence on plantation agriculture.

10. Most migrants to the West claimed free land under the provisions of the 1862 Homestead Act.

11. Western agriculture experienced the same trend toward consolidation that occurred in the manufacturing and industrial sector.

12. Between 1870 and 1900, 60 to 70 percent of the nation's workers were manual laborers.

13. Most steelworkers in the late nineteenth century worked at least seventy-two hours per week.

14. In 1880, about three-quarters of all immigrants to the United States came from southern and eastern Europe.

15. In the late nineteenth and early twentieth centuries, about half of all manual wage earners advanced into middle-class jobs.

SOURCES FOR FURTHER RESEARCH

Books

Edward Ayers, *The Promise of the New South* (1992).
Alfred D. Chandler Jr., *The Visible Hand: The Managerial Revolution in American Business* (1977).
Roger Daniels, *Coming to America: A History of Immigration and Ethnicity in American Life* (1990).
Alice Kessler-Harris, *Out to Work: A History of Wage-Earning Women in the United States* (1982).
Alexander Keyssar, *Out of Work: The First Century of Unemployment in Massachusetts* (1986).
Patricia Nelson Limerick, *Legacy of Conquest: The Unbroken Past of the American West* (1987).
David F. Noble, *America by Design: Science, Technology, and the Rise of Corporate Capitalism* (1977).
Alan Trachtenberg, *The Incorporation of America: Culture and Society in the Gilded Age* (1982).
Richard White, *It's Your Misfortune and None of My Own: A History of the American West* (1991).
Olivier Zunz, *Making America Corporate, 1870–1920* (1990).

Videos

The Richest Man in the World: Andrew Carnegie (120 minutes, PBS Video, 1997). This documentary, originally produced for *The American Experience,* follows Carnegie's life from his impoverished origins in Dunfermline, Scotland, through his business career, where he was on the cutting edge of the industrial revolution in steel.

The Telephone (60 minutes, PBS Home Video, 1997). Using photos and archival sound and film footage, this video tells the story of the invention of the telephone, from the earliest instruments to the first coast-to-coast call. It also explores the telephone's impact on American life.

Edison's Miracle of Light (59 minutes, PBS Video, 1990). This video, originally broadcast as part of the PBS series *The American Experience,* tells the story of Thomas Edison's invention of the lightbulb and his subsequent battle with George Westinghouse over the type of electric current to be used. It also discusses the launching of the Edison General Electric Company.

The Iron Road (58 minutes, PBS Video, 1990). This video, originally broadcast as part of the PBS series *The American Experience,* documents the building of the first transcontinental railroad. It took 20,000 men, including 10,000 Chinese immigrants, six years to build 1,700 miles of track stretching from Omaha to Sacramento. The completion of the railroad reduced the cross-country trip from several months to just nine and a half days, united the state of California with the rest of the United States, and brought about a wave of western expansion.

The West: The Grandest Enterprise Under God (84 minutes, West Film Project/WETA, 1996). After the Civil War, Americans set out to unite the East and West by building the first transcontinental railroad. The herding of cattle and the hunting of buffalo also became prevalent in this period. This video is episode five in Ken Burns's nine-part series on the American West.

Hester Street (89 minutes, Midwest Film Production, 1974). This tale, set in the melting pot of New York's Lower East Side, explores the trials and tribulations encountered by a young immigrant couple as they discard their Old World traditions and adjust to life in America. When Gitl joins her husband at Ellis Island, she finds that he has already become an "American," forsaken old customs, and, much to her dismay, fallen in love with a "modern" American woman.

Journey to America (59 minutes, PBS Video, 1990). This video, originally broadcast as part of the PBS series *The American Experience,* offers a tribute to the over 12 million men, women and children who arrived at New York's Ellis Island between 1890 and 1920.

Web Resources

The Society for Historians of the Gilded Age and Progressive Era offers a general guide to Internet resources on the rise of big business, the transformation of the West, American workers, and the new immigration.
        http://www2.h-net.msu.edu/~shgape/internet/index.html

The University of Colorado at Colorado Springs hosts a similar site at
        http://web.uccs.edu/~history/index/shgape.html#general.

The Library of Congress's "American Memory" project offers "Inside an American Factory: Films of the Westinghouse Works, 1904." The collection contains twenty-one "actuality" films showing various views of Westinghouse companies. Most prominently featured are the Westinghouse Air Brake Company, the Westinghouse Electric and Manufacturing Company, and the Westinghouse Machine

Company. The films were intended to showcase the company's operations. Exterior and interior shots of the factories are shown along with scenes of male and female workers performing their duties. The website also includes additional material on the company and working conditions in the plants.

http://memory.loc.gov/ammem/papr/west/westhome.html

The "Thomas Edison Papers" website, hosted by Rutgers University, offers a wealth of information and primary sources on Edison and his inventions.

http://edison.rutgers.edu.

The John W. Hartman Center for Sales, Advertising, and Marketing History at Duke University offers a website detailing "The Emergence of Advertising, 1850–1920." The site presents over 9,000 images, which provide a significant and informative perspective on the early evolution of this most ubiquitous feature of modern American business and culture.

http://scriptorium.lib.duke.edu/eaa

"WestWeb" is a topically organized website about the history of the American West.

http://www.library.csi.cuny.edu/westweb

Information on the "new immigrants" can be found at the website of the Ellis Island Immigration Museum.

http://www.ellisisland.com

An Industrial Society: 1870–1910

CHAPTER OBJECTIVES

- Describe the reasons for, and consequences of, the "integration" of American society in the decades following the Civil War.
- Discuss the treatment accorded southern blacks, Native Americans, and immigrants in the late nineteenth and early twentieth centuries.
- Describe the changes and continuities that the emergence of an industrial society brought to farm life.
- Explain the explosive growth of cities between 1870 and 1910, and detail the opportunities and problems that came with urban growth.
- Describe the ways in which the emerging industrial society changed women's lives.
- Explain how the triumph of industrial capitalism and the emergence of modern science (particularly Darwin's theory of evolution) changed the way Americans viewed their world between 1860 and 1900.

CHAPTER OUTLINE

I. Integration and Segmentation
   A. National Integration
      1) Examples and reasons
         a) mail and telegraph
         b) common habits and consumer goods
         c) mobility
      2) Erosion of local communities
      3) Nationalization of work and social life
   B. The Jim Crow South
      1) White actions

          a)   increasing de facto and de jure segregation
          b)   lynching and other anti-black violence
      2)   African American reaction
          a)   resistance vs. acquiescence
          b)   Booker T. Washington
          c)   W. E. B. Du Bois
      3)   Supreme Court upholds segregation

  C. Reforming Native Americans
      1)   The "Peace Policy"
          a)   stress on civilization and Christianization
          b)   upsurge in war on the Great Plains
          c)   destruction of the buffalo
      2)   Assimilation Policy
          a)   elements of the policy
          b)   benefits settlers and railroad corporations more than Indians
      3)   Emerging belief in the biological inferiority of Indians leads to second-class citizenship

  D. Strangers in the Land
      1)   Mixed reaction of native-born Americans to immigrants
      2)   Hostility directed toward non-European immigrants
          a)   Chinese
          b)   Japanese
          c)   Mexicans
      3)   Nativism directed at European immigrants
          a)   fear of radicals and union organizers
          b)   anti-Catholicism
          c)   fear of "race suicide" and the eugenics movement

II. Life on the Farm
  A. Changes
      1)   New markets
      2)   Technological innovations reduce drudgery, increase productivity
      3)   More contact with urban world
      4)   Mail-order catalogs change consumption patterns
  B. Continuities
      1)   Seasonal rhythms
      2)   Gendered division of labor
  C. Regional Variations
      1)   Great Plains
      2)   The South
  D. Migration to Cities
      1)   Push factors
      2)   Pull factors

III. The Rise of the City
  A. An Urban Society

   1) Explosive growth of cities
   2) Types of cities
     a) metropolises
     b) "specialist" cities
  B. Cities and Technology
   1) New modes of transportation
     a) horse-drawn streetcars
     b) elevated trains
     c) cable cars
     d) electrified streetcars
     e) subways
   2) Bridges
   3) The "balloon frame" house
   4) Streetcar suburbs
  C. The Immigrant City
   1) Living conditions in ethnic neighborhoods
     a) overcrowding
     b) disease
     c) unsteady, low-wage work
   2) Social life
     a) community-wide organizations
     b) men and saloons
     c) women
     d) children
  D. The City of Lights
   1) Downtowns
     a) skyscrapers
     b) department stores
   2) Improvements in physical infrastructure
     a) electric lighting
     b) paved streets
     c) water and sewer lines
  E. Public Health and the City of Disease
   1) Infectious diseases and death rates
   2) "Anticontagionists"
   3) Scientific medicine
IV. Women in Industrial Society
  A. Education
   1) More women attend high school and college
   2) Reasons
  B. Work
   1) Rise in participation in paid labor force
   2) Reasons
   3) Cultural resistance

   C. Family
- 1) Declining fertility rates
- 2) Tighter abortion and birth control laws
- 3) Impact of new household technologies

   D. The New Woman
- 1) Clubs and associations
- 2) Women's Christian Temperance Union

V. The World Viewed

   A. Education
- 1) Public schools
- 2) Kindergartens
- 3) Universities

   B. Science and Society
- 1) Charles Darwin's *Origin of Species*
  - a) challenge to religious views of the world
  - b) model of an empirical approach to knowledge
- 2) Social Darwinism and its critics
  - a) Herbert Spencer
  - b) William Graham Sumner
  - c) Frank Lester Ward
- 3) Intellectual approaches to industrialization and political unrest
- 4) Debates over gender and racial inequality

   C. Religion
- 1) A potent force
- 2) The challenge of Darwinism
  - a) Protestant conservatives vs. modernists
  - b) Reform Jewish reaction
  - c) Christian Scientists
- 3) The challenge of industrial capitalism
  - a) Gospel of Wealth
  - b) Social Gospel
  - c) Jewish and Catholic reactions

   D. Law, Philosophy, Art
- 1) Oliver Wendell Holmes and the law
- 2) Pragmatic philosophers: William James and John Dewey
- 3) Realism in art and literature
- 4) The emergence of cultural hierarchy

CHRONOLOGY

1872–74	The great buffalo slaughter on the Great Plains.
1873	San Francisco builds first cable car line.

	Women's Christian Temperance Union founded.
	Comstock Law passed.
1874	Black Hills gold rush begins.
1876	Custer's defeat at the Battle of Little Bighorn.
	Johns Hopkins University opens nation's first graduate school.
1878	Yellow fever epidemic in Memphis.
1879	Henry George publishes *Progress and Poverty.*
	Mary Baker Eddy founds the Church of Christ, Scientist.
1881	Booker T. Washington founds the Tuskegee Institute.
1882	Congress passes Chinese Exclusion Act.
1883	Supreme Court rules Civil Rights Act of 1875 unenforceable.
	Brooklyn Bridge completed.
1885	William Dean Howells publishes *The Rise of Silas Lapham.*
	World's first skyscraper, the Home Life Insurance Building, built in Chicago.
1886	Haymarket Affair fuels nativism.
1887	Dawes Severalty Act passed.
	American Protective Association founded.
1888	First electrified streetcar system begins operation in Richmond, Virginia.
	Edward Bellamy publishes *Looking Backward.*
1890	Jacob Riis publishes *How the Other Half Lives.*
1893	New York City aqueduct completed.
1895	Booker T. Washington gives Atlanta Compromise speech.
1896	Free rural mail delivery begins.
	Supreme Court upholds segregation in *Plessy v. Ferguson* decision.
1897	Boston opens first subway line.
1898	White race riot in Wilmington, North Carolina.
1909	W. E. B. Du Bois and others found the National Association for the Advancement of Colored People.
1924	Citizenship conferred upon all Native Americans.

ESSAY QUESTIONS

1. The decades following the Civil War saw the "integration" and nationalization of American society. What factors contributed to these developments?

How might the life of someone living in a rural area have been different as a result of nationalizing trends?

2. How did race relations in the South change between the end of Reconstruction and 1900? What similarities and differences do you see between the treatment of African Americans in the South and Native Americans in the West?

3. How and why did urban life change during the late nineteenth century? How did the lifestyles of middle-class and working-class urbanites differ? What common problems did they face?

4. In what ways would a woman's life in 1910 have been similar to or different from her grandmother's life in 1865? Discuss living conditions and everyday life, as well as opportunities for work and social activism available to women.

5. In the decades following the end of the Civil War, Darwin's theories of evolution and natural selection cast a long shadow over intellectual and social thought in the United States. Explain how evolutionary theories shaped debates and cultural thought about business and government regulation, gender and racial inequality, religion, law, and philosophy.

OBJECTIVE QUESTIONS

Multiple Choice

1. The "integration" and nationalization of American society after the Civil War was hastened by:
   a) the introduction of free mail delivery
   b) mass production and distribution of consumer products and goods
   c) unprecedented population mobility
   d) all of the above

2. Many southern blacks did not oppose the imposition of "Jim Crow" laws in the late nineteenth and early twentieth centuries because:
   a) the Supreme Court quickly struck down such laws
   b) they feared economic or violent reprisals by whites
   c) they preferred not to mingle with whites if possible
   d) all of the above

3. W. E. B. Du Bois achieved fame:
   a) for his delivery of the "Atlanta Compromise" address in 1895
   b) as the primary spokesman for the Niagara movement, which advocated the militant pursuit of legal, economic, and political equality for blacks
   c) as the editor of the *Boston Guardian*
   d) for challenging segregation aboard Louisiana railroad cars

4. The phrase "Talented Tenth" refers to:
   a) a group of educated blacks who would both set an example to whites and also agitate to improve the conditions of other African Americans
   b) Native American graduates of boarding schools set up by Christian reformers
   c) Chinese immigrants who managed to overcome white hostility and succeed by opening laundries and restaurants in the West
   d) the "old stock" Americans whom many social scientists feared were threatened by the immigration of "degenerate breeding stock" from southern and eastern Europe

5. The Dawes Severalty Act of 1887:
   a) permitted individual Indians to acquire title to allotments of reservation land
   b) granted some Native Americans U.S. citizenship
   c) primarily benefited settlers and railroad corporations
   d) all of the above

6. During the late nineteenth century and early twentieth centuries, all of the following opposed immigration except:
   a) industrialists
   b) trade unionists
   c) many middle-class Protestants
   d) Boston Brahmins

7. During the late nineteenth century, the lives of rural farm families were altered most by:
   a) changing gender roles
   b) mail-order catalogs
   c) the establishment of the National Weather Bureau
   d) the growth of rural townships

8. All of the following cities were "specialist" cities except:
   a) Sacramento, California
   b) Philadelphia, Pennsylvania
   c) Richmond, Virginia
   d) Columbus, Ohio

9. Saloons were vital to working-class life in American cities because they:
   a) offered customers free hot meals
   b) gave men a social space in which to unwind and form friendships
   c) cashed checks
   d) all of the above

10. Electricity:
    a) made possible the development of subways
    b) contributed to the spread of skyscrapers in American cities

    c)   allowed businesses to stay open longer
    d)   all of the above

11. "Anticontagionists":
    a)   believed that germs and bacteria were the primary cause of disease
    b)   worked to clean up streets and construct city sewer systems
    c)   led to widespread middle-class embrace of public health measures
    d)   all of the above

12. The lives of middle-class women changed markedly in the late nineteenth and early twentieth centuries as a result of:
    a)   the loosening of laws banning birth control and abortion
    b)   the introduction of new household technologies, which gave housewives more free time
    c)   the proliferation of women's clubs and associations
    d)   all of the above

13. The spread of kindergartens and public schools in the late nineteenth and early twentieth centuries reflected all of the following except:
    a)   a democratic desire to provide universal education for all children
    b)   industry's need for a skilled and disciplined labor force
    c)   the rising number of women in the workforce, combined with the lack of appropriate daycare
    d)   a desire to reduce friction between people of diverse backgrounds and beliefs

14. The foremost American advocate of Social Darwinism was:
    a)   John Dewey
    b)   Herbert Spencer
    c)   William Graham Sumner
    d)   Frank Lester Ward

15. Those who subscribed to the Social Gospel believed that:
    a)   prosperity and high social status were signs of divine favor
    b)   Christians should work to rectify social injustice
    c)   sin and vice were personal deficiencies
    d)   the working poor would be saved by the church, not by political action

True or False

1. Most southern states introduced legally mandated segregation immediately following the Civil War.

2. The former slave Booker T. Washington argued that blacks should "glorify common labor" and accept social segregation.

3. The "Peace Policy" which shaped federal relations with Native Americans in late 1860s and 1870s reflected the belief of many eastern reformers that Indians belonged to an inferior race.

4. Like Chinese immigrants and many Native Americans, Mexican immigrants were denied U.S. citizenship in the late nineteenth and early twentieth centuries.

5. Eugenicists like Madison Grant favored selective breeding of the human race.

6. In 1910, most inhabitants of northeastern cities came from surrounding farms and rural areas.

7. The development of electric streetcars was a major factor in the growth of suburbs in the late nineteenth and early twentieth centuries.

8. "Dumbbell tenements," which had windows in every room, greatly improved living conditions for most tenement dwellers.

9. In Chicago's "Packingtown" district, more than half of all families took in boarders.

10. In the 1880s, tuberculosis killed roughly one in every eight Americans.

11. Between 1870 and 1920, more men than women graduated from high school.

12. After 1870, states in all parts of the country adopted laws making school attendance mandatory.

13. The field of sociology emerged from turn-of-the-century efforts to study society scientifically.

14. Christian Scientists believed that the sick should use modern medicine to supplement prayer and meditation.

15. The pragmatic philosopher John Dewey believed that truth could be discovered only through experimentation.

SOURCES FOR FURTHER RESEARCH

Books

Edward Ayers, *The Promise of the New South: Life After Reconstruction* (1992).
John Bodnar, *The Transplanted: A History of Immigrants in Urban America* (1985).
Charles W. Calhoun, ed., *The Gilded Age: Essays on the Origins of Modern America* (1996).
William Cronon, *Nature's Metropolis: Chicago and the Great West* (1991).
Susan Curtis, *A Consuming Faith: The Social Gospel and Modern American Culture* (1991).

Roger Daniels, *Coming to America: A History of Immigration and Ethnicity in American Life* (1990).

Barbara Leslie Epstein, *The Politics of Domesticity: Women, Evangelism, and Temperance in Nineteenth-Century America* (1981).

Lisa M. Fine, *The Souls of the Skyscraper: Female Clerical Workers in Chicago, 1870–1930* (1990).

John Higham, *Strangers in the Land: Patterns of American Nativism, 1860–1925* (1955).

Frederick E. Hoxie, *A Final Promise: The Campaign to Assimilate the Indians, 1880–1920* (1984).

Kenneth T. Jackson, *Crabgrass Frontier: The Suburbanization of the United States* (1985).

Daniel J. Kevles, *In the Name of Eugenics: Genetics and the Uses of Human Heredity* (1985).

Lawrence W. Levine, *Highbrow/Lowbrow: The Emergence of Cultural Hierarchy in America* (1988).

Joanne J. Meyerowitz, *Women Adrift: Independent Wage Earners in Chicago, 1880–1930* (1988).

Kathy Peiss, *Cheap Amusements: Working Women and Leisure in Turn-of-the-Century New York* (1986).

John R. Stilgoe, *Borderland: Origins of the American Suburb, 1820–1939.*

Alan Trachtenberg, *The Incorporation of America: Culture and Society in the Gilded Age* (1982)..

Robert Utley, *The Indian Frontier of the American West, 1846–1890* (1984).

Sam B. Warner Jr., *Streetcar Suburbs: The Process of Growth in Boston, 1870–1900* (1962).

Morton Gabriel White, *Social Thought in America: The Revolt Against Formalism* (1949).

C. Vann Woodward, *The Strange Career of Jim Crow*, 3rd rev. ed. (1974).

Videos

America, 1900 (170 minutes, PBS Video, 1998). Using archival film and photographs, and interviews with historians, writers, and descendants, this film looks back at the year 1900. It features President McKinley's reelection; the guerrilla war in the Philippines; John Muir's nature movement; inventions such as motion pictures, X-rays, automobiles, phonographs, electric lights, and indoor plumbing; the Gibson Girl; photojournalist Frances Benjamin Johnston; public morality and Olga Nethersole's play *Sapho*; huge waves of immigration; the deadly coal mine explosion in Scofield, Utah; racism and Jim Crow in the South; the attempts of U.S. Congressman George White of North Carolina to outlaw lynching; black leaders Booker T. Washington and W. E. B. Du Bois; Scott Joplin and the birth of the music industry; China's Boxer Rebellion and the fate of missionaries like Eva,

Charles, and Florence Price; the deadly hurricane that hit Galveston, Texas; John Mitchell's attempts to unite coal workers; and the United Mine Workers strike.

New York: A Documentary Film: Episode Three, Sunshine and Shadow, 1865–1898 (115 minutes, PBS Video, 1999). This Ric Burns film, originally broadcast as part of the series *The American Experience,* shows how Gilded Age New York was becoming increasingly divided between the haves (the Robber Barons) and the have-nots (tenement dwellers). The video also details the rise and fall of "Boss" Tweed; the financial crisis of 1873, which set the stage for an economic rebirth masterminded by J. P. Morgan; the construction of the Brooklyn Bridge; and the plight of the poor as documented by Jacob Riis.

New York Underground (60 minutes, PBS Video, 1999). This video, originally broadcast as part of the series *The American Experience,* tells the story of how the longest, most sophisticated electric subway in the world was built. Interviews with experts on nineteenth-century technology and New York social history discuss how the construction dramatically changed New York City.

The Gilded Age (58 minutes, PBS Video, 1996). This video, part of the eight-part *American Visions* television special, examines the many sides of American art and design in the nineteenth century: the extravagant mansions of Newport's tycoons; the triumph of the Brooklyn Bridge; the haunting realism of Civil War photography; and the artistic creations of John Singer Sargent, James Whistler, Mary Cassatt, Augustus Saint-Gaudens, Thomas Eakins, John Peto, Winslow Homer, John Robling, Louis Sullivan, Isabella Stewart Gardner, and Bernard Berenson.

Web Resources

The Society for Historians of the Gilded Age and Progressive Era offers a general guide to Internet resources on the Gilded Age.
        http://www2.h-net.msu.edu/~shgape/internet/index.html

The University of Colorado at Colorado Springs hosts a similar site.
        http://web.uccs.edu/~history/index/shgape.html#general

"African-American Perspectives, Pamphlets from the Daniel A. P. Murray Collection, 1818–1907," a website created by the Library of Congress, reviews almost one hundred years of African American history from the early nineteenth through the early twentieth centuries, with the bulk of the material published between 1875 and 1900. Among the authors represented are Frederick Douglass, Booker T. Washington, Ida B. Wells-Barnett, Benjamin W. Arnett, Alexander Crummel, and Emanuel Love. The website also includes a timeline of African American history from 1852 to 1925.
        http://lcweb2.loc.gov/ammem/aap

Photographs and postcards taken as souvenirs at lynchings throughout America were displayed at the New York Historical Society and collected in the book *Without Sanctuary*. These images can now be viewed on-line. Students should be aware that much of the material on this site is very disturbing.

> http://www.journale.com/withoutsanctuary/main.html

Information on the "new immigrants" and the hostility they faced can be found at the website of the Ellis Island Immigration Museum.

> http://www.ellisisland.com

Hypertext of Jacob Riis's *How the Other Half Lives* (1890), complete with illustrations, can be found at

> http://www.cis.yale.edu/amstud/inforev/riis/title.html.

An on-line collection of documents dating from the late nineteenth and early twentieth century about slum conditions in New York City can be found at

> http://140.190.128.190/history/hours10.html.

Images from *The Ram's Horn,* an interdenominational Social Gospel magazine that was published in Chicago from the 1890s through the early twentieth century, can be found on a site hosted by Ohio State University. The cartoons and illustrations presented reveal Social Gospel attitudes toward such topics as immigrants, the wealthy, liquor, trusts, and political bosses.

> http://www.cohums.ohio-state.edu/history/projects/Ram's_Horn

| Politics and the State: 1876–1900

CHAPTER OBJECTIVES

- Describe how public authorities at all levels (city, state, and national) responded to the problems of industrialization and urbanization during the Gilded Age. Assess their ability to deal with these problems.
- Discuss the reasons workers turned to national unions in the decades following the Civil War, as well as the differing political and organizational strategies of the National Labor Union, the Knights of Labor, and the American Federation of Labor. Also discuss other strategies used by workers, including political parties and strikes.
- Detail the progress of the women's suffrage movement between Reconstruction and 1900, including changing arguments for and against women's suffrage.
- Outline the constituencies of the two major parties during the Gilded Age, as well as their positions on key issues.
- Describe the major causes and consequences of the Populist movement of the 1880s and 1890s, as well as the reasons for its ultimate demise.
- Discuss the concept of "laissez-faire constitutionalism," and explain how it was applied by federal judges in the late nineteenth century.

CHAPTER OUTLINE

I. Rule and Misrule in the Cities
    A. Critics and Challenges
    B. Political Machines
        1) General characteristics
    C. Boss Tweed
        1) The Tweed Ring

          a)   fraud and corruption
          b)   accomplishments
   D. Other Centers of Power
       1) Mayors
       2) Experts
       3) State governments
   E. Divided Rule
       1) Successes
          a)   enlargement of municipal services
          b)   creation of physical infrastructure
          c)   debt reduction
       2) Failures
          a)   private property regulation
          b)   meeting the material needs of the poor

II. Statehouses and Legislatures
   A. State Activism
       1) Regulation of financial and transportation sectors
       2) Aiding agriculture
       3) Social reforms
       4) Prohibition and "local option"
   B. Massachusetts and Unemployment
       1) Investigation of the problem
       2) Response
   C. Characteristics of State Politics
       1) Strong party organizations in some states
       2) High voter turnout
       3) Strong party allegiances
   D. The South
       1) Less activism
       2) The politics of race
          a)   fiercely contested elections through the 1880s
          b)   legal disfranchisement

III. The Politics of Insurgency
   A. Labor Uniting
       1) National Unions
          a)   National Labor Union
          b)   Knights of Labor
          c)   American Federation of Labor
       2) Politics and Strikes
          a)   political parties
          b)   Great Railroad Strike of 1877
          c)   Haymarket Square bombing
          d)   Pullman Strike
   B. Women's Suffrage

       1) Setbacks during Reconstruction
       2) National women's suffrage organizations
       3) Ideological sources of resistance to women's suffrage
          a) harmful to women and family life
          b) declining faith in democracy
       4) Shifting arguments in favor of women's suffrage
       5) Impact of the movement during the Gilded Age
  C. Farmers and Their Discontents
       1) Discontents
       2) The Grange
       3) Farmers' Alliances
          a) agenda
          b) 1890 political campaign
IV. The Nation State
  A. Parties and Issues
       1) Regional and class constituencies
       2) Issues
          a) the tariff
          b) civil service reform
          c) the money question
          d) regulating business
          e) the South and the nation
  B. Presidential Politics, 1877–1892
       1) Hayes, Garfield, and Arthur
       2) Cleveland and Harrison
  C. The People's Party and the Election of 1892
       1) The Omaha Platform
       2) Challenges facing the People's Party
       3) Populist successes
  D. The Crisis of the 1890s
       1) The depression of 1893
       2) Cleveland's response
       3) Midterm elections of 1894
  E. The Election of 1896
       1) Republicans nominate William McKinley
       2) Democrats nominate William Jennings Bryan
       3) Populists opt for "fusion"
       4) The campaign
       5) Reasons for Bryan's defeat
       6) Impact of Bryan's defeat
V. The Conservative Courts
  A. Makeup of the Federal Courts
  B. Laissez-Faire Constitutionalism
       1) Labor law

      2)   Government regulation
VI. The New Political Universe
    A. Single-Party Dominance
    B. Decline in Participation
    C. Declining Visibility of Third Parties

CHRONOLOGY

1866	National Labor Union founded.
1867	National Grange of the Patrons of Husbandry founded.
1868	Fourteenth Amendment explicitly restricts suffrage to males.
1869	Knights of Labor founded.
1873	Congress passes the Coinage Act, terminating the minting of silver dollars.
1874	Greenback Party organized.
1875	Congress passes the Resumption Act. Supreme Court rules in *Minor v. Happersett* that right to vote is not inherent in citizenship.
1877	The Great Railroad Strike of 1877. Southern Farmers Alliance organized. Supreme Court decides *Munn v. Illinois.*
1881	President James Garfield assassinated. Chester Arthur sworn in.
1883	Congress passes the Pendleton Act, creating a Civil Service Commission.
1885	First appearance in print of the word "unemployment."
1886	American Federation of Labor founded. May Day strike for the eight-hour workday. Haymarket Square bombing.
1887	Congress passes the Interstate Commerce Act.
1890s	Southern states pass laws aimed at disfranchising blacks.
1890	National American Woman's Suffrage Association founded. Congress passes the Sherman Silver Purchase Act. Congress passes the Sherman Anti-Trust Act.
1892	Formation of the People's Party. Grover Cleveland elected president.
1893	Congress repeals all laws authorizing federal supervision of southern elections. Panic of 1893 triggers severe depression. Sherman Silver Purchase Act repealed.

1894	Pullman Strike.
1895	Supreme Court issues three decisions—*U.S. v. E.C. Knight, In Re Debs,* and *Pollack v. Farmers' Loan and Trust Co.*—restricting state regulatory laws.
1896	William McKinley defeats William Jennings Bryan to win presidency.
1900	Congress passes Gold Standard Act.

ESSAY QUESTIONS

1. Why did the president of Cornell University in 1890 declare U.S. city governments to be "the worst in Christendom"? Do you agree with this assessment? Justify your answer, paying attention to both their achievements and their failures.

2. How did state governments respond to the problems of urbanization and industrialization during the Gilded Age? How did these responses vary from region to region? Were they successful?

3. Compare the goals and strategies of the Knights of Labor and the American Federation of Labor. Why did the American Federation of Labor survive, while the once-successful Knights of Labor foundered?

4. During the late nineteenth century, African Americans, women, and immigrant workers faced mounting campaigns to keep them away from the ballot box. Describe these various efforts at disfranchisement, as well as the tactics used by blacks, women, and immigrants to retain or attain a measure of political representation.

5. What were the major causes and consequences of the Populist movement of the 1880s and 1890s? Why do historians consider the election of 1896 to be a watershed in American politics?

OBJECTIVE QUESTIONS

Multiple Choice

1. National politics had a humdrum flavor during the "Gilded Age" because:
   a) the capacities of the state to act were limited
   b) public authorities faced few pressing problems
   c) there was widespread agreement on how most problems should be solved
   d) all of the above

2. In the 1860s and 1870s, the political machine of William Marcy Tweed:
    a) won political elections in part by hiring "repeaters"
    b) used kickbacks to loot the public treasury
    c) distributed meals, cash, fuel and other services to the poor
    d) all of the above

3. During the Gilded Age, U.S. senators were elected by:
    a) the voters in each state
    b) state legislators
    c) statewide political machines
    d) conventions of state delegates

4. In the late nineteenth century, city governments responded to the problems of industrialization and urbanization by:
    a) building physical infrastructure
    b) turning to experts
    c) nurturing machine politicians who were attuned to the needs of working-class immigrants and their children
    d) all of the above

5. In the late nineteenth century, the percentage of Massachusetts industrial workers who were unemployed for at least part of any given year was:
    a) 5 percent
    b) 10 percent
    c) 20 percent
    d) 30 percent

6. Beginning in the 1880s, southern states used all of the following methods to keep blacks from voting except:
    a) campaigns of violence and intimidation
    b) denying their citizenship
    c) literacy tests
    d) poll taxes

7. The leader of the Knights of Labor was:
    a) Terence V. Powderly
    b) Jay Gould
    c) Samuel Gompers
    d) Eugene Debs

8. The Haymarket Square bombing, which led to the rigged trial and conviction of eight radicals in Chicago, occurred in:
    a) 1869
    b) 1877
    c) 1886
    d) 1894

9. The Pullman Strike:

    a)   soon spread beyond the workers who manufactured Pullman sleeping cars

    b)   prompted President Cleveland to use federal troops to suppress the strike

    c)   ultimately led to the formation of the Socialist Party of America

    d)   all of the above

10. In the late nineteenth century, all of the following arguments were used by proponents of federal women's suffrage except:
    a) women's special talents and qualities would help clean up the world of politics
    b) enfranchising women would offset the menace posed by poor, immigrant, and black male voters
    c) many states had already granted women the right to vote
    d) politically engaged women would be more interesting wives and better mothers

11. In the late nineteenth century, the percentage of federal revenues derived from tariffs was:
    a) less than 10 percent
    b) 20 percent
    c) 35 percent
    d) often more than 50 percent

12. During the late nineteenth century, the federal government used all of the following instruments to intervene in the economy except:
    a) control over the money supply
    b) income taxes
    c) tariffs
    d) direct regulation of business practices

13. The liberal, northeastern Republicans who advocated civil service reform were known as:
    a) Fusionists
    b) Mugwumps
    c) Stalwarts
    d) Half-breeds

14. The People's Party advocated all of the following policies except:
    a) government ownership of the railroads and telegraph
    b) free coinage of silver
    c) open immigration
    d) direct election of senators

15. The election of 1896 was noteworthy because:
    a) the Democrats and Populists nominated the same candidate
    b) the Republicans raised an unprecedented amount of money from corporations
    c) it marked the end of the Gilded Age era of divided government
    d) all of the above

True or False

1. The Scottish political observer James Bryce believed that the "one conspicuous failure of the United States" was the gap between rich and poor.

2. Most urban political machines in the late nineteenth century were Democratic.

3. In the late nineteenth century, most big-city mayors emerged from the same world of ethnic, ward politics that produced political bosses.

4. During the Gilded Age, Methodists were most likely to support the Democrats.

5. Laws adopted by southern legislatures to keep blacks from voting also disenfranchised many poor whites.

6. During the late nineteenth century, labor unions tended to fare best during periods of economic depression.

7. The American Federation of Labor and its affiliated unions welcomed to their ranks "all producers," including unskilled workers, women, and blacks.

8. During the Gilded Age, advocates of women's suffrage frequently made common cause with advocates of black voting rights.

9. Advocates of "resumption" in the late nineteenth century were most often Republicans.

10. In 1884, Grover Cleveland became the first Democrat elected to the presidency since the Civil War.

11. In his famous "Cross of Gold" speech, William Jennings Bryan advocated a return to the gold standard.

12. In 1896, many southern Populists welcomed the chance to "fuse" with the Democratic Party.

13. In 1896, William Jennings Bryan failed to win the votes of urban, ethnic workers in the Northeast and Midwest.

14. The Fourteenth Amendment was originally intended to protect the rights of freed slaves, but during the Gilded Age courts increasingly used it to protect corporations.

15. In most states, voter turnout rates were higher in 1896 than in 1920.

SOURCES FOR FURTHER RESEARCH

Books

Leon Fink, *Workingmen's Democracy: The Knights of Labor and American Politics* (1983).

Eleanor Flexnor, *Century of Struggle: The Women's Rights Movement in the United States* (1975).

Morton Keller, *Affairs of the State: Public Life in Late Nineteenth Century America* (1988).

Alexander Keyssar, *Out of Work: The First Century of Unemployment in Massachusetts* (1986).

J. Morgan Kousser, *The Shaping of Southern Politics: Suffrage Restriction and the Establishment of a One-Party South* (1974).

Nell Irvin Painter, *Standing at Armageddon: The United States, 1877–1919* (1987).

Seymour J. Mandelbaum, *Boss Tweed's New York* (1965).

Robert C. McMath, *American Populism: A Social History* (1993).

David Montgomery, *The Fall of the House of Labor: The Workplace, the State, and American Labor Activism, 1865–1925* (1987).

Louise Michele Newman, *White Women's Rights: The Racial Origins of Feminism in the United States* (1999).

Richard Schneirov, Shelton Stromquist, and Nick Salvatore, eds., *The Pullman Strike and the Crisis of the 1890s: Essays on Labor and Politics* (1999).

Jon C. Teaford, *The Unheralded Triumph: City Government in America, 1870–1900* (1983).

C. Vann Woodward, *The Strange Career of Jim Crow*, 3rd rev. ed. (1974).

Videos

Not for Ourselves Alone: The Story of Elizabeth Cady Stanton and Susan B. Anthony (210 minutes, PBS Video, 1999). This video tells the story of the friendship and work of these two suffragists.

One Woman, One Vote (114 minutes, PBS Video, 1995). Documents the seventy-year struggle for women's suffrage that culminated in the ratification of the Nineteenth Amendment in 1920. The film illuminates the alliances, betrayals, and defeats that paved the way for victory in the battle for women's right to vote.

Web Resources

The Society for Historians of the Gilded Age and Progressive Era offers a general guide to Internet resources on the Gilded Age.
http://www2.h-net.msu.edu/~shgape/internet/index.html

The University of Colorado at Colorado Springs hosts a similar site at
http://web.uccs.edu/~history/index/shgape.html#general.

"The Haymarket Affair Digital Collection," created by the Chicago Historical Society, provides on-line access to the Society's primary sources related to this pivotal episode in American labor history.
http://www.chicagohistory.org/hadc/index.html

In-depth analysis of the history of the Haymarket Affair can be found at "The Dramas of Haymarket," an affiliated, interpretive website developed by Northwestern University in cooperation with the Chicago Historical Society.

http://www.chicagohistory.org/dramas

The Library of Congress hosts two useful sites on women's suffrage: "Votes for Women: Selections from the National American Woman Suffrage Association Collection, 1848–1921"

http://memory.loc.gov/ammem/naw/nawshome.html

and "By Popular Demand: 'Votes for Women' Suffrage Pictures, 1850–1920"

http://memory.loc.gov/ammem/vfwhtml/vfwhome.html.

The White House sponsors a website that contains biographical information on all of the Gilded Age presidents.

http://www.whitehouse.gov:80/history/presidents/filmore-mckinley.html

The text of William Jennings Bryan's famous "Cross of Gold" speech can be found at

http://douglass.speech.nwu.edu/brya_a26.htm.

Vassar College hosts a website devoted to the cartoons and commentary of the 1896 presidential campaign. In addition to hundreds of political cartoons, the website contains a chronology of events, information on political leaders and campaign themes, and state-by-state election results.

http://iberia.vassar.edu/1896/1896home.html

CHAPTER 21

A New Place in the World: 1865–1914

CHAPTER OBJECTIVES

- Identify the traditional impulses that shaped U.S. foreign policy in the half-century following the Civil War, as well as the new factors that increasingly prompted Americans to turn their gaze abroad.
- Discuss the causes and consequences of the Spanish-American War.
- Outline the arguments made around the turn of the century by both anti-imperialists and those who favored U.S. expansion overseas.
- Compare and contrast the diplomatic tactics used by the United States in various parts of the world, notably the Caribbean, Central and South America, the Pacific, and the Far East, and indicate any changes over time.
- Describe and assess the foreign policy approaches of Theodore Roosevelt, William Howard Taft, and Woodrow Wilson.

CHAPTER OUTLINE

I. The United States' Changing Global Role: An Overview
    A. The United States in 1870
    B. The United States in 1914
II. Postbellum Stirrings, 1865–1890
    A. Traditional Impulses Shaped U.S. Foreign Policy
        1) Expansionism
        2) Isolationism
        3) Anti-colonialism
    B. William Henry Seward: Expansionist Visionary
        1) From a territorial to a commercial vision
        2) Alaska and the Midway Islands
        3) Congressional resistance

    C. Factors Prompting Americans to Look Abroad
       1) Economic issues
          a) rising domestic productivity
          b) perceived need for foreign markets
          c) foreign investments and investors
          d) immigrant workers
       2) Technological advances
          a) faster ships and railroads
          b) trans-Atlantic cable
          c) quinine
       3) Ideology
          a) the "closing" of the western frontier
          b) social Darwinism
       4) Pressure from U.S. expatriots
          a) Minor Keith and the United Fruit Company
          b) Hawaiian planters
    D. Continuing Resistance
    E. The Old Army and the New Navy
       1) Army is slow to embrace new technology
       2) Navy begins to modernize
III. Turning Point: The 1890s
    A. Sources of the New Expansionism
       1) Increasingly heated competition for empire
       2) Rebellious subjects
       3) Fears of domestic overproduction
       4) Convictions about American "specialness"
    B. Britain, the Monroe Doctrine, and the Venezuela Crisis
       1) Developments
       2) Significance
    C. Cuba and War with Spain
       1) Cuban rebellion
       2) Growing economic ties between Cuba and the United States
       3) Spain's policy of *reconcentrado*
       4) Americans debate intervention
       5) Explosion of the *Maine* and the drumbeat for war
    D. The United States at War
       1) America's shifting military strategy
       2) Untrained troops, poor equipment, and unsanitary conditions
       3) U.S. victory in Cuba
       4) Americans seize Puerto Rico
    E. Conquering the Philippines
       1) United States seizes Manila
       2) United States annexes Hawaii

3) Anti-imperialist sentiment
4) Congress ratifies treaty with Spain

F. Suppressing Revolution in the Philippines
1) United States refuses to recognize nationalist government
2) A long and costly war

G. Legacies
1) Ruling the new possessions
a) Cuba
b) Puerto Rico
c) the Philippines
2) Modernizing the army and navy

IV. The New Century

A. The Open Door to China
1) Hay's first "Open Door Note"
2) Boxer Rebellion and Hay's second "Open Door Note"
3) Impact on presidential election of 1900

B. The Panama Canal
1) The case for a canal
2) Choosing a site
3) Diplomatic dealings
4) Construction of the canal

C. The Roosevelt Corollary
1) The Roosevelt Corollary
a) Roosevelt shifts American policy
b) application in the Dominican Republic
2) Racial and cultural condescension
3) Dealings with Japan
a) Russo-Japanese War
b) Gentlemen's Agreement

D. Dollar Diplomacy and Wilsonian Idealism
1) Taft and "dollar diplomacy"
2) Wilson's missionary vision
3) U.S. interventions under Wilson
a) Nicaragua
b) Haiti
c) Dominican Republic
d) Mexico

V. A New Empire

CHRONOLOGY

1866	Trans-Atlantic cable completed.
1867	United States purchases Alaska from Russia.

1868	Cuban nationalists launch war for independence.
1875	United States eliminates tariffs on Hawaiian sugar.
1887	United States acquires rights to use Pearl Harbor as a naval base.
1890	Alfred Thayer Mahan publishes *The Influence of Sea Power Upon History.*
1895	Venezuela Crisis.
1896	William McKinley defeats William Jennings Bryan for president. Spain sends troops to Cuba; launches *reconcentrado* policy.
1898	Explosion of the *Maine* and start of the Spanish-American War. Annexation of Hawaii. Anti-Imperialist League formed.
1899	Filipino nationalists declare war on the United States. Secretary of State John Hay sends his first "Open Door Note."
1900	Foraker Act declares Puerto Rico an "unincorporated territory" of the United States. China's Boxer Rebellion prompts Hay's second "Open Door Note." President McKinley wins reelection.
1901	Platt amendment grants Cuba independence, with strings attached. Supreme Court rules in the *Insular Cases.* Assassination of President McKinley; Teddy Roosevelt becomes president.
1902	Most Filipino rebels surrender to the United States.
1903	Panama declares independence.
1904	Senate approves construction of the Panama Canal. President Roosevelt issues the Roosevelt Corollary.
1905	President Roosevelt mediates the Russo-Japanese War.
1907	The "Gentlemen's Agreement" ends Japanese immigration to the United States.
1913	Completion of the Panama Canal.
1914	American forces occupy Vera Cruz, Mexico.
1915	United States sends marines into Haiti; occupation lasts until 1934.
1916	United States sends marines into the Dominican Republic. Punitive Expedition pursues Pancho Villa into Mexico.
1917	Puerto Ricans become citizens of the United States.

ESSAY QUESTIONS

1. Discuss the relationship between American economic interests and U.S. expansionism around the turn of the century. Make sure to distinguish between formal imperialism and other forms of expansionism.

2. Who were the anti-imperialists, and what were their primary arguments before, during, and immediately after the Spanish-American War? Did they share any common ground with those who favored U.S. imperialism?

3. Compare the United States' goals and strategies in its dealings with Cuba, the Philippines, Hawaii, China, and Panama. How successful was it in each of these arenas?

4. What role did scientific and technological advances play in shaping U.S. expansionism between 1890 and 1916? How might the nation's global role have been different were it not for these breakthroughs? Be sure to cite specific examples.

5. Discuss the Roosevelt corollary, as well as specific examples of its application by both Theodore Roosevelt and Woodrow Wilson. To what degree did it represent a continuation of, or shift in, American foreign policy?

OBJECTIVE QUESTIONS

Multiple Choice

1. "Seward's Folly" referred to Secretary of State William Henry Seward's plan to:
   a) erect a commercial "highway" to Asia
   b) purchase Alaska from Russia
   c) build a canal across Panama
   d) annex the Dominican Republic

2. All of the following contributed to Americans' growing interest and involvement in overseas affairs during the 1880s and 1890s except:
   a) rising domestic productivity
   b) the activities of companies controlled by Americans living abroad
   c) the discovery of new uses for quinine
   d) the United States' geographic isolation

3. All of the following favored U.S. expansionism in the 1880s and 1890s except:
   a) Minor Keith
   b) Alfred Thayer Mahan
   c) William Jennings Bryan
   d) Henry Cabot Lodge

4. The Venezuela Crisis of 1895 marked a turning point in global politics because:
   a) the United States acquired an area rich in gold
   b) the United States went to war with Britain for the third time in its history
   c) the British tacitly recognized U.S. hegemony in the western hemisphere
   d) Venezuela became a U.S. protectorate

5. Spain's policy of *reconcentrado:*
   a) was politically ineffective
   b) led to the deaths of more than 200,000 Cubans
   c) was repeated by the United States in the Philippines
   d) all of the above

6. The United States declared war against Spain:
   a) within a week of the explosion of the battleship *Maine*
   b) on behalf of the Cuban nationalists
   c) only after disclaiming any desire to take over control of Cuba
   d) all of the above

7. Anti-imperialists argued that:
   a) acquiring overseas territory would not necessarily open markets abroad
   b) the United States lacked the constitutional right to acquire colonies
   c) imperialism would subvert American democracy
   d) all of the above

8. By 1900, the United States controlled all of the following except:
   a) Cuba
   b) Puerto Rico
   c) the Philippines
   d) Hawaii

9. The United States' war against Filipino nationalists:
   a) was the United States' first war of counterinsurgency
   b) involved more than 120,000 U.S. troops
   c) prompted American troops to resort to brutal tactics
   d) all of the above

10. Cuba was granted formal independence, but given limited autonomy, by:
    a) the Teller amendment
    b) the Platt amendment
    c) the Foraker Act
    d) the Dick Act

11. In the three years following the Spanish-American War, the United States' military budget:
    a) fell by 25 percent
    b) remained stable

c) doubled

d) rose by more than 300 percent

12. The "Boxers" were a militant, anti-foreign group in:
   a) China
   b) the Philippines
   c) Hawaii
   d) Puerto Rico

13. "You have shown that you were accused of seduction and you have conclusively proved that you were guilty of rape." Secretary of War Elihu Root made this statement in response to:
   a) President McKinley's decision to wage war against the Philippine nationalists
   b) John Hay's response to the Boxer Rebellion
   c) Teddy Roosevelt's dealings with Panama and Colombia in connection with the Panama Canal
   d) Woodrow Wilson's intervention in the Dominican Republic

14. During Woodrow Wilson's presidency, the United States intervened in all of the following countries except:
   a) Nicaragua
   b) Venezuela
   c) Haiti
   d) Mexico

15. The Mexican revolutionary who led raids across the U.S. border in 1915 and 1916 was:
   a) Jose Marti
   b) Porfirio Diaz
   c) Venustiano Carranza
   d) Pancho Villa

True or False

1. American expansionists believed in Anglo-Saxon racial superiority, while anti-imperialists generally shunned such beliefs.

2. As railroad construction slowed in the 1890s, U.S. steel makers became increasingly dependent on orders from the navy.

3. Secretary of State John Hay's "splendid little war" was waged against nationalist rebels in the Philippines.

4. President Grover Cleveland favored U.S. intervention in Cuba, but met with resistance from Congressional Democrats.

5. Most men who served in the U.S. Army during the Spanish-American War were volunteers.

6. Andrew Carnegie offered to buy the Philippines for $20 million because he hoped to set up his own colony.

7. Emilio Aguinaldo was the leader of the revolutionary forces in the Philippines.

8. The U.S. Army used strategies developed fighting Native Americans to defeat the Filipino rebels.

9. Puerto Ricans became citizens in 1900 with the passage of the Foraker Act.

10. The "Open Door Notes" were drafted by Secretary of State John Hay.

11. The number of workers who died constructing the Panama Canal exceeded the number of American soldiers who died in Cuba, Puerto Rico, and the Philippines combined.

12. President Roosevelt believed that both the Chinese and the Japanese belonged to "backwards" peoples.

13. The "Gentlemen's Agreement" called for all industrial nations to have equal trading rights in China.

14. "Dollar diplomacy" was a term coined to describe the foreign policy of Woodrow Wilson.

15. The U.S. Army first used aircraft to support its military operations in 1916.

SOURCES FOR FURTHER RESEARCH

Books

Robert L. Beisner, *From the Old Diplomacy to the New, 1865–1900* (2nd ed., 1986).

H.W. Brands, *Bound to Empire: The United States and the Philippines* (1992).

Lewis L. Gould, *The Spanish-American War and President McKinley* (1982).

David Healy, *Drive to Hegemony: The United States in the Caribbean, 1888–1917* (1988).

Michael H. Hunt, *Ideology and U.S. Foreign Policy* (1987).

Amy Kaplan and Donald E. Pease, eds., *Cultures of United States Imperialism* (1993).

Walter LaFeber, *The New Empire: An Interpretation of American Expansion, 1860–1898* (1963; rev. ed. 1998).

———, *The American Search for Opportunity, 1865–1913* (1993).

Ernest R. May, *Imperial Democracy: The Emergence of America as a Great Power* (1961; reprint ed. 1973).

David McCullough, *Path Between the Seas: The Creation of the Panama Canal, 1870–1913* (1977).

Stuart Creighton Miller, *"Benevolent Assimilation": The American Conquest of the Philippines, 1899–1903* (1982; reprint ed., 1984).

John L. Offner, *An Unwanted War: The Diplomacy of the United States and Spain over Cuba, 1895–1898* (1992).

Emily S. Rosenberg, *Spreading the American Dream: American Economic and Cultural Expansion, 1890–1945* (1982).

Anders Stephanson, *Manifest Destiny: American Expansion and the Empire of the Right* (1995).

William Appleman Williams, *The Tragedy of American Diplomacy* (1959).

Videos

America, 1900 (170 minutes, PBS Video, 1998). Using archival film and photographs, and interviews with historians, writers, and descendants, this film looks back at the year 1900. It features President McKinley's reelection; the guerrilla war in the Philippines; John Muir's nature movement; inventions such as motion pictures, X-rays, automobiles, phonographs, electric lights, and indoor plumbing; the Gibson Girl; photojournalist Frances Benjamin Johnston; public morality and Olga Nethersole's play *Sapho*; huge waves of immigration; the deadly coal mine explosion in Scofield, Utah; racism and Jim Crow in the South; the attempts of U.S. Congressman George White of North Carolina to outlaw lynching; black leaders Booker T. Washington and W. E. B. Du Bois; Scott Joplin and the birth of the music industry; China's Boxer Rebellion and the fate of missionaries like Eva, Charles, and Florence Price; the deadly hurricane that hit Galveston, Texas; John Mitchell's attempts to unite coal workers; and the United Mine Workers strike.

Crucible of Empire: The Spanish-American War (120 minutes, PBS Video, 1999). This video examines the colorful characters and historic events surrounding the Spanish-American War and its relevance through the twentieth century. Using reenactments, interviews with noted authors and popular historians, and more than a dozen newly arranged popular songs from the period, *Crucible of Empire* looks at the influence of race, economics, new technologies, and the news media on America's decision to go to war.

The American President: The World Stage (54 minutes, PBS Video, 2000). Episode six in PBS's series *The American President,* this video examines the president's greatest responsibility: representing the nation on the world stage. From the very beginning, securing a stable world in which American interests can be defended and asserted has been a basic part of the presidency. The episode profiles William McKinley and Woodrow Wilson, as well as James Monroe and George Bush.

Latin America: Intervention in Our Own Backyard (25 minutes, PBS Video, 1978). Explores early U.S. policy in the Caribbean and Central and South America as Pan-American relations deteriorated until, in 1933, President Roosevelt abolished the Monroe doctrine of intervention.

TR and His Times (58 minutes, PBS Video, 1983). This video, originally broadcast as part of the series *A Walk Through the Twentieth Century with Bill Moyers,* looks at Theodore Roosevelt and the role he played in helping to shape America at the turn of the century. With his energy and optimism, Roosevelt successfully ushered the country onto the world stage and championed reform legislation, setting a precedent for a strong chief executive.

TR: The Story of Theodore Roosevelt (240 minutes, PBS Video, 1996). A biography of Teddy Roosevelt, originally broadcast as part of *The American Experience* series.

"Remember the Maine": The Roots of the Spanish-American War (50 minutes, Films for the Humanities and Sciences, 1998). Using archival footage, newspaper excerpts, and historical documents, this program traces the roots of the Spanish-American War to Spain's quest to preserve its flagging empire, American imperialism, and the genuine desire on the part of Cubans to shake off the yoke of Spanish domination. It closely examines the role of Cuba's poet/patriot Jose Marti, exposes American expansionist policies that contributed to our decision to enter the war, and reveals Spanish attempts to thwart open conflict.

Web Resources

The Society for Historians of the Gilded Age and Progressive Era offers a general guide to Internet resources on the Gilded Age and Progressive Era, including the Spanish-American War and its aftermath.
> http://www2.hnet.msu.edu/~shgape/internet/index.html

The University of Colorado at Colorado Springs hosts a similar site.
> http://web.uccs.edu/~history/index/shgape.html#general.

The Hispanic Division of the Library of Congress offers "The World of 1898: The Spanish-American War." The site provides resources and documents about the Spanish-American War, the period before the war, and some of the people who participated in the fighting or commented about it. Information about Cuba, Guam, the Philippines, Puerto Rico, Spain, and the United States is provided in chronologies, bibliographies, and a variety of pictorial and textual materials from bilingual sources, supplemented by an overview essay about the war and the period.
> http://lcweb.loc.gov/rr/hispanic/1898/index.html

"The Spanish-American War in Motion Pictures," presented by the Library of Congress's "American Memory" project, features sixty-eight motion pictures produced between 1898 and 1901 of the Spanish-American War and the subsequent Philippine Revolution. The Spanish-American War was the first U.S. war in which the motion picture camera played a role. These films were made by the Edison Manufacturing Company and the American Mutoscope & Biograph Company and were filmed in the United States, Cuba, and the Philippines. They show troops, ships, notable figures, and parades, as well as reenactments of battles and other wartime events. The motion pictures are presented in chronological order together with brief essays that provide a historical context for their filming.

http://memory.loc.gov/ammem/sawhtml/sawhome.html

"A War in Perspective, 1898–1998: Public Appeals, Memory, and the Spanish-American Conflict" is an on-line version of an exhibit presented by the New York Public Library.

http://www.nypl.org/research/chss/epo/spanexhib/index.html

"Anti-Imperialism in the United States, 1898–1935" reproduces anti-imperialist writings and cartoons by Mark Twain, William Dean Howells, William Jennings Bryan, Andrew Carnegie, Samuel Gompers, and many others.

http://www.boondocksnet.com/index.html

"Stereoscopic Visions of War and Empire" is an interpretive archive of 3-D stereoscopic photographs of the Spanish-American and Philippine-American wars, the colonies acquired by the United States at the turn of the century, and other representations of imperialism and empires produced at the end of the nineteenth century and first decades of the twentieth. The site contains more than 400 images, including many from Cuba, the Philippines, Puerto Rico, Panama, Hawaii, Samoa, Guam, and China during the Boxer Rebellion.

http://www.boondocksnet.com/stereo/index.html

CHAPTER 22 | The Progressive Era: 1900–1916

CHAPTER OBJECTIVES

- Outline the factors that contributed to the United States' economic boom between 1900 and 1920, and describe the impact of technological systems like electricity and the automobile on Americans during this period.
- Characterize the Progressive Era, and describe its different manifestations at the local, state, and national levels.
- Discuss the variety of Progressive approaches to the problems of workers, immigrants, African Americans, and large corporations.
- Discuss the role of women in Progressive reform movements, as well as the impact such movements had on women's lives.
- Compare the approaches and accomplishments of the three Progressive presidents: Theodore Roosevelt, William Howard Taft, and Woodrow Wilson.
- Assess the legacies of the Progressive Era.

CHAPTER OUTLINE

I. America at the Dawn of the Twentieth Century
    A. An Unfinished Agenda
    B. The Progressive Temper
       1) Optimism
       2) Empiricism
       3) Pragmatism
       4) Activist government
    C. The Era of Electricity and the Automobile
II. A Growing Economy
    A. Overview
       1) Steady growth
       2) Uneven growth

B. Immigration Reconsidered
   1) The immigration "problem"
      a) labor competition
      b) the changing urban landscape
      c) politics
   2) Responses of the native-born
      a) Americanization programs
      b) violence and discrimination
      c) eugenics and fears of "race suicide"
      d) immigration restrictions
C. Race and the Nation
   1) Race relations in the South
      a) Jim Crow laws and other legal restrictions
      b) disfranchisement continues
   2) Blacks migrate to the urban North
   3) African Americans' reception in the North
      a) marginalization and discrimination
      b) black ghettoes
      c) racial violence
VI. Women and Reform
   A. Jobs and Rights
      1) Jobs and education
         a) the continuing ideal of domesticity
         b) working-class women
         c) middle-class women
      2) Women and social reform
         a) Ida B. Wells-Barnett and antilynching
         b) Margaret Sanger and birth control
         c) S. Josephine Baker and public health
         d) Charlotte Perkins Gilman and the emergence of "feminism"
      3) Legislative victories
      4) Full equality vs. protection
   B. Winning the Right to Vote
      1) The "doldrums"
      2) The National American Woman Suffrage Association
         a) an ideological shift
         b) scattered victories
         c) opponents
      3) Pursuing a constitutional amendment
         a) organizing and protests
         b) World War I: the turning point
         c) ratification of the Nineteenth Amendment
VII. National Politics

A. The Presidential Election of 1900
    1) William Jennings Bryan emphasizes foreign policy
    2) Central issues: currency and the tariff
    3) McKinley wins
B. The Roosevelt Era
    1) McKinley's assassination
    2) Roosevelt's personality and views
    3) Roosevelt's first term
       a) trust-busting
       b) labor: the anthracite coal strike
       c) conservation
    4) The election of 1904
    5) Roosevelt's second term
       a) the "monopoly" question
       b) regulating the railroads
       c) regulating food and drugs
       d) onset of political gridlock
C. The Successor: William H. Taft
    1) The election of 1908
    2) Legislative successes
    3) Setbacks
       a) Pinchot-Ballinger controversy erupts
       b) formation of the Progressive Republican League
D. The Election of 1912
    1) The contenders
       a) Republicans renominate Taft
       b) Teddy Roosevelt leads the Progressive Party
       c) Democrats nominate Woodrow Wilson
    2) The campaign
       a) "New Nationalism" vs. "New Freedom"
       b) Wilson emerges victorious
E. Wilson: The Scholar as President
    1) Legislative successes
       a) tariff revision
       b) banking reform
       c) antitrust policy
       d) labor law
       e) Louis Brandeis and the Supreme Court
    2) The election of 1916
F. The Legacy of Reform
    1) The end of the "progressive" era
    2) Legislative achievements and limitations
    3) The scaffolding of the modern American state
    4) Legitimizing reform

CHRONOLOGY

1889	Jane Addams founds Hull House.
1894	Immigration Restriction League founded.
1896	Henry Ford builds his first automobile.
1898	Charlotte Perkins Gilman publishes *Women and Economics.*
1900	Galveston, Texas, creates first city commission government. William McKinley wins reelection. Progressive Robert La Follette is elected governor of Wisconsin.
1901	Congress creates the National Bureau of Standards. McKinley is assassinated; Theodore Roosevelt becomes president.
1902	Theodore Roosevelt mediates anthracite coal strike. Congress passes the Newlands Reclamation Act.
1904	Supreme Court finds Northern Securities Company in violation of the Sherman Anti-Trust Act. Creation of the Commerce Department. Roosevelt proclaims "Square Deal"; wins reelection.
1905	Albert Einstein publishes special theory of relativity. Industrial Workers of the World founded. Roosevelt creates the U.S. Forest Service.
1906	Passage of the Hepburn Act. Upton Sinclair publishes *The Jungle.* Passage of the Pure Food and Drug and Meat Inspection Acts.
1907	Immigration to the United States peaks at 1.2 million.
1908	Ford Motor Company introduces the Model T. In *Muller v. Oregon,* Supreme Court upholds restricted hours for female workers. William Howard Taft elected president.
1909	Ballinger-Pinchot controversy.
1911	Frederick Winslow Taylor publishes *The Principles of Scientific Management.*
1912	IWW leads textile strike in Lawrence, Massachusetts. Woodrow Wilson elected president.
1913	Ford adopts the moving assembly line. Ratification of the Sixteenth Amendment (federal income tax). Ratification of the Seventeenth Amendment (direct election of senators). Federal Reserve Act passed. Underwood-Simmons Tariff passed.

1914	Clayton Anti-Trust Act passed.
1916	Madison Grant publishes *The Passing of the Great Race.* Wilson appoints Louis Brandeis to the Supreme Court.
1919	Ratification of the Eighteenth Amendment (prohibition).
1920	Ratification of the Nineteenth Amendment (women's suffrage).
1924	National Origins Act drastically restricts immigration to the United States.

ESSAY QUESTIONS

1. How did new technologies and scientific approaches affect the lives of Americans in the first two decades of the twentieth century? Consider differences in the experiences of industrial workers, farmers, and middle-class urbanites.

2. Compare the Populist movement of the 1890s with Progressive reform efforts. (Refer to Chapter 20, if necessary.) What similarities and differences do you see between the supporters of the two movements, their reform agendas and strategies, and their impact on American society and politics?

3. Discuss the role of women reformers during the Progressive Era, giving specific examples. What issues seemed most urgent to them, and how did they go about effecting change? Were all female Progressives feminists?

4. Compare the political agendas and styles of Theodore Roosevelt and Woodrow Wilson. In what ways was each man conservative or reform-oriented? Who was more successful?

5. What was the lasting impact of the Progressive Era? How did the United States in 1920 look different from the United States in 1900?

OBJECTIVE QUESTIONS

Multiple Choice

1. Between 1900 and 1920, farm incomes rose for all of the following reasons except:
   a) a dramatic increase in cultivated acreage
   b) higher prices for farm products
   c) the development of gas-powered tractors
   d) improved variants of corn and wheat

2. By 1920, the percentage of U.S. homes wired for electricity was roughly:
   a) 20 percent
   b) 33 percent

c) 50 percent
d) 75 percent

3. Henry Ford introduced the Model T in:
   a) 1896
   b) 1903
   c) 1908
   d) 1917

4. The moving assembly line:
   a) forced employees to work at a pre-set rhythm
   b) helped small automobile makers become more profitable
   c) was eagerly embraced by industrial workers
   d) all of the above

5. Hull House was founded by:
   a) Margaret Sanger
   b) Jane Addams
   c) S. Josephine Baker
   d) Charlotte Perkins Gilman

6. The state whose progressive reform efforts offered a blueprint for others was:
   a) New York
   b) Massachusetts
   c) Wisconsin
   d) California

7. Support for prohibition was strong:
   a) among evangelical Protestants
   b) in rural areas
   c) in the South and West
   d) all of the above

8. The Industrial Workers of the World were led by:
   a) Samuel Gompers
   b) "Big" Bill Haywood
   c) Eugene Debs
   d) Victor Berger

9. Of the following immigrants, the most likely to remain in the United States was:
   a) an Italian day laborer
   b) a Japanese farm worker
   c) a Jewish garment worker
   d) a Polish meatpacker

10. By 1920, most women employed outside their own home were:
    a) domestic servants

b) clerical workers
c) teachers
d) garment workers

11. The Eighteenth Amendment to the Constitution:
    a) allowed the federal government to collect income taxes
    b) called for the popular election of senators
    c) prohibited the manufacture, sale, and transportation of alcohol
    d) gave women the right to vote

12. President Roosevelt's greatest policy innovations came in the area of:
    a) trust-busting
    b) labor law
    c) conservation
    d) railroad regulation

13. Upton Sinclair's muckracking novel *The Jungle* helped rally popular support for:
    a) the Elkins Act
    b) the Newlands Reclamation Act
    c) the Hepburn Act
    d) the Meat Inspection Act

14. In the presidential election of 1912, Teddy Roosevelt called his campaign platform:
    a) the Square Deal
    b) the New Nationalism
    c) the New Freedom
    d) the Fair Deal

15. The Adamson Act:
    a) lowered most tariffs by roughly 25 percent
    b) created a national banking system
    c) established the Federal Trade Commission
    d) mandated an eight-hour workday on railroads

True or False

1. Between 1900 and 1920, the United States' gross national product grew faster than the population.

2. Industries in the eastern United States were more likely to be located along rivers than those in the western United States.

3. In 1920, public utilities supplied most of the electricity in the United States.

4. Frederick Winslow Taylor coined the phrase "scientific management" to describe the new breed of engineers who ran the nation's industrial research labs.

5. Progressive reformers believed that Darwinian evolution would solve the nation's most pressing problems.

6. The city manager system weakened the political influence of ethnic workers.

7. In the presidential election of 1912, the Socialist Party's candidate garnered 6 percent of all votes cast.

8. In 1910, a majority of the inhabitants in the nation's largest cities were immigrants or their children.

9. Trade unionists generally opposed restrictions on immigration.

10. When African Americans migrated north, they escaped problems of racial segregation.

11. Opponents of prohibition generally opposed women's suffrage as well.

12. Both Woodrow Wilson and Teddy Roosevelt agreed that only "unreasonable" restraints of trade were illegal.

13. In the election of 1912, the Republican Party's candidate, William Howard Taft, came in second.

14. Some business leaders supported the Clayton Anti-Trust Act.

15. During the Progressive Era, the federal government came to rely increasingly on income taxes for its revenue.

SOURCES FOR FURTHER RESEARCH

Books

Jane Addams, *Twenty Years at Hull House* (1910).
Paula Baker, *The Moral Frameworks of Public Life* (1991).
Stewart Bird, Dan Georgakas, Deborah Shaffer, eds., *Solidarity Forever: An Oral History of the IWW* (1985).
John Morton Blum, *The Progressive Presidents* (1980).
Paul Boyer, *Urban Masses and Moral Order in America, 1820–1920* (1978).
Mina Carson, *Settlement Folk: Social Thought and the American Settlement Movement, 1885–1930* (1990).
Ellen Chesler, *Woman of Valor: Margaret Sanger and the Birth Control Movement in America* (1992).
John Milton Cooper Jr., *The Warrior and the Priest: Theodore Roosevelt and Woodrow Wilson* (1983).
———, *The Pivotal Decades, 1900–1920* (1990).
Ruth Schwartz Cowan, *A Social History of American Technology* (1996).

Eldon J. Eisenach, *The Lost Promise of Progressivism* (1994).
Ellen Fitzpatrick, *Endless Crusade: Women Social Scientists and Progressive Reform* (1990).
Glenda Gilmore, *Gender and Jim Crow: Women and the Politics of White Supremacy in North Carolina, 1896–1920* (1996).
Daniel J. Kevles, *In the Name of Eugenics: Genetics and the Uses of Human Heredity* (1985).
Alexander Keyssar, *The Right to Vote: The Contested History of Democracy in the United States* (2000).
James T. Kloppenberg, *Uncertain Victory: Social Democracy and Progressivism in European and American Thought, 1870–1920* (1986).
David E. Nye, *Electrifying America: Social Meanings of a New Technology, 1880–1940* (1990).
Nick Salvatore, *Eugene V. Debs* (1982).
Upton Sinclair, *The Jungle* (1906).
Bernard A. Weisberger, *The La Follettes of Wisconsin* (1994).
Robert H. Wiebe, *The Search for Order* (1967).

Videos

Ida B. Wells: A Passion for Justice (58 minutes, PBS Video, 1989). This video, originally produced for *The American Experience,* chronicles the life of Ida B. Wells, an African American activist who protested lynchings, unfair treatment of black soldiers, and other examples of racism and injustice toward black Americans around the turn of the century. Born into slavery in a small town in Mississippi, Wells became a school teacher and journalist. She was shocked into action following the lynching of three of her friends, and commenced a lifelong crusade against racism, sexism, and other indignities. Her antilynching campaign took her to the capitals of urban America and Europe.

Margaret Sanger (87 minutes, Films for the Humanities, 1997). Margaret Sanger was a birth control advocate, self-styled libertarian, and ardent proponent of women's rights. Using rare archival footage, diary excerpts, and commentary from historians, critics, and relatives, the program traces Sanger's extraordinary life and exhaustive work in the promotion and legalization of contraception. The documentary examines Sanger's legal battles, her work to distribute scientific birth control information, and her best-known achievement: the establishment of Planned Parenthood. Grandson Alexander Sanger offers insight into her Bohemian life as well as the fierce oppposition she faced from conservative religious and social groups. Margaret Sanger is seen in both triumph and failure. At the start of her career, she opened the first birth control clinic in the United States. She finished her work a half century later after launching the research that led to the birth control pill. But her darker side—her use of the racist and elitist language of eugenics—haunts her memory to this day.

TR and His Times (58 minutes, PBS Video, 1983). Originally part of the series *A Walk Through the Twentieth Century with Bill Moyers,* this video explores the way Theodore Roosevelt helped shape America at the turn of the century. With his energy and optimism, Roosevelt successfully ushered the country onto the world stage and championed reform legislation, setting a precedent for a strong chief executive.

On the Line, 1924 (57 minutes, PBS Video, 1999). This video, originally broadcast as part of the *People's Century* series, discusses the implementation of mass production and how it altered workers' relationship to their product. Focusing on the Ford Motor Company, it examines the advent of assembly lines and how the men who worked on them formed labor unions.

The Lynchburg Story (55 minutes, Filmakers Library, 1993). This video charts the history of the American eugenics program under which 80,000 inmates in state institutions were compulsorily sterilized. In Virginia between 1905 and 1972, several thousand children deemed by the state as unfit to reproduce were taken from their families and forced to live in the Lynchburg Colony. Victims recall their experiences of beatings, solitary confinement, and other abuses.

New York: A Documentary Film: Episode Four, The Power and the People, 1898–1918 (120 minutes, Warner Home Video/PBS Home Video, 1999). In the fourth episode of this series chronicling the history of New York, the forces of capitalism and democracy come to a stunning crescendo. The city's industrial engine draws in people from around the world, tripling New York's population within a single lifetime. The film climaxes with the 1911 fire at the Triangle Shirtwaist Factory Fire that killed 146 workers and spurred a wave of Progressive reform legislation.

Eugene Debs and the American Movement (44 minutes, Cambridge Documentary Films, 1979). A biographical sketch of Eugene V. Debs, labor leader, industrial unionist, and American Socialist, narrated by his friend and comrade Shubert Sebree. This video shows strikes and government repression of workers' attempts to organize, and highlights the difference between progressivism and socialism.

Web Resources

The Society for Historians of the Gilded Age and Progressive Era offers a general guide to Internet resources on "Progressive Reform, 1900–1917."
        http://www2.h-net.msu.edu/~shgape/internet/index.html

An invaluable insight into the Industrial Workers of the World ("Wobblies") can be gleaned from a University of Arizona website that presents numerous pamphlets produced by the radical unionists. Documents include the IWW's preamble and constitution, an IWW poster warning against U.S. involvement in World War I, pamphlets explaining the uses of sabotage, and an IWW songbook.
        http://digital.library.arizona.edu/bisbee/main/iww.php

"The Triangle Factory Fire," a presentation of the Kheel Center for Labor-Management Documentation and Archives at Cornell University, tells the story of one of the worst workplace disasters ever. The 1911 fire at the Triangle Shirtwaist Company in New York City claimed the lives of 146 young immigrants, highlighted the miserable working conditions to which many unskilled workers were subjected, and resulted in the passage of important factory safety legislation. In addition to the story of the fire and its aftermath, the website offers a bibliography and an array of primary sources: worker testimonials, newspaper accounts, the text of ballads written to commemorate the event, photographs, political cartoons, and reports of the commission established to investigate the fire.
http://www.ilr.cornell.edu/trianglefire/default.html

The Library of Congress hosts two useful sites on women's suffrage: "Votes for Women: Selections from the National American Woman Suffrage Association Collection, 1848–1921"
http://memory.loc.gov/ammem/naw/nawshome.html
and "By Popular Demand: 'Votes for Women' Suffrage Pictures, 1850–1920"
http://memory.loc.gov/ammem/vfwhtml/vfwhome.html.

The Margaret Sanger Papers Project at New York University presents documents that chronicle Sanger's publication of the radical feminist journal *The Woman Rebel* and her emergence as the foremost leader of the birth control movement. The events surrounding the publication of *The Woman Rebel* in 1914—including Sanger's indictment for violation of federal obscenity laws, her unlawful flight from prosecution, her thirteen months in exile in Europe, and her emotional return to New York in the fall of 1915 to face trial—trace the inception of the birth control movement in the United States and mark a pivotal time in Sanger's life. *The Woman Rebel* established Sanger as a dynamic and controversial feminist voice, the leading birth control agitator in America, and an influential international leader, a position she held for the next fifty years. Readers can jump directly from a document image to brief biographies of individuals addressed in the document, descriptions of relevant organizations mentioned in the document, texts of the laws involved, and a chronology.
http://www.nyu.edu/projects/sanger/index.html

"The Evolution of the Conservation Movement, 1850–1920," part of the Library of Congress's "American Memory" project, documents the historical formation and cultural foundations of the movement to conserve and protect America's natural heritage, through books, pamphlets, government documents, manuscripts, prints, photographs, and motion picture footage. The site offers a wealth of material on President Roosevelt's conservation policies, as well as writings by John Muir, Gifford Pinchot, and others.
http://memory.loc.gov/ammem/amrvhtml/conshome.html

Ohio State University presents "1912: Competing Visions for America," an online guide to the candidates and issues confronting Americans in the 1912 presidential election. Using the election campaign as a launching pad, the site explores issues that were at the heart of national debates during the Progressive Era: Should America be capitalist or socialist? Should government protect the social welfare of citizens? Should women vote? Should government exercise more control over business? Should government try to resolve the conflict between "capital" and "labor"? Should government work vigorously for the conservation of natural resources?

http://1912.history.ohio-state.edu

CHAPTER 23 | War, Prosperity, and the Metropolis: 1914–1929

CHAPTER OBJECTIVES

- Understand the reasons for the outbreak of World War I, as well as the causes and consequences of U.S. involvement in the war.
- Discuss the United States' retreat from internationalism in the wake of World War I.
- Characterize and assess the political philosophies and policies of Presidents Harding, Coolidge, and Hoover.
- Analyze the strengths and weaknesses of the American economy in the 1920s.
- Describe metropolitan life in America during the Jazz Age, and outline the key cultural divides of the decade.
- Understand the key issues in the election of 1928 and describe the election's outcome.

CHAPTER OUTLINE

I. Introduction
II. The Road to War
    A. The Strains of Neutrality
        1) U-boat attacks on Allied shipping
        2) Sinking of the *Lusitania*
    B. Peace and Preparedness
        1) Divided public opinion
        2) U.S. loans to the Allies
        3) Wilson's reelection
    C. Entry into the War
        1) Germany's stepped-up U-boat attacks

2) The Zimmerman telegram
3) U.S. declaration of war
III. Prosecuting the War
   A. Initial Lack of Preparedness
   B. Financing the War
      1) Taxation
      2) "Liberty Loans"
   C. War Production
      1) Mobilization strategies
         a) reliance on big business
         b) voluntarism
         c) federal management
      2) The Food Administration
      3) Prohibition
      4) Long-term impact of federal intervention
   D. Science to the Front
   E. Into Combat
      1) Allied weakness
      2) The Russian Revolution
      3) The convoy
      4) Selective service
      5) The American Expeditionary Force
      6) Costs
         a) low U.S. casualty rate
         b) Spanish influenza
         c) shell shock
   F. Wartime Society
      1) A booming economy
         a) economic indicators
         b) labor
         c) business
      2) African Americans
         a) migration north
         b) racial tensions
         c) military service
      3) Women
         a) new employment opportunities
         b) suffrage
      4) Assaults on civil liberties
         a) Committee on Public Information
         b) anti-Germanism and anti-immigrant sentiment
         c) Espionage and Sedition Acts
         d) repression of dissent
IV. Retreat from Internationalism

A. Ending the War
    1) Wilson's "Fourteen Points"
    2) The armistice
B. The Versailles Peace Conference
    1) Treaty of Versailles
    2) Treaty of Sevres and Balfour Declaration
    3) Analysis of the terms of peace
    4) Allied intervention in Russia
C. Battle over the League of Nations
    1) Opposition in the Senate
    2) Wilson's collapse
    3) Failure to ratify the Versailles Treaty
    4) Treaty of Berlin
D. Unrest and Reaction
    1) Demobilization and labor strife
    2) Racial and ethnic tensions
    3) The Red Scare
        a) anarchist bombings
        b) the Palmer raids
        c) rising xenophobia
E. Republican Reign
    1) The election of 1920
    2) Harding, then Coolidge
        a) Harding's brief tenure
        b) Coolidge and the election of 1924
        c) pro-business conservatism
F. Foreign Affairs
    1) Military research and development (R&D)
    2) Washington Arms Limitation Conference
    3) Kellogg-Briand Pact
    4) Dealings with Latin America
    5) A private internationalism
V. A Prosperous Nation
  A. Construction
  B. The Auto Industry
    1) Technological advances
    2) Ford's competitors
    3) Highway improvements
    4) Fueling economic growth
  C. Appliances and Radio
    1) Electrification
    2) Appliance industry
    3) Radio
  D. Flaws in the Economy

        1) Redistribution of wealth upward
        2) Labor
            a) weakness of unions
            b) welfare capitalism
            c) conditions of assembly line work
        3) Agriculture
            a) economic woes
            b) rise of agribusiness
            c) overproduction
            d) farm life
    E. Metropolitan Life
        1) The growth of suburbia
            a) accelerated by car ownership
            b) congestion and parking problems
            c) impact on cities
        2) Mass media
            a) radio
            b) movies
            c) newspapers
            d) celebrities
        3) Consumerism
            a) advertising
            b) impact of Prohibition
        4) Health, public and private
            a) sanitation, medical advances, and child development
            b) eugenics
VI. The Jazz Age
    A. Cultural Ferment
        1) Writers and readers
        2) Painters
        3) Criticism of urban technological civilization
    B. The Vitality of Science
        1) Artists' fascination with science and technology
        2) Robert Millikan
        3) University science
    C. Blacks in the Cities
        1) The Great Migration
        2) Marcus Garvey and the UNIA
        3) The Harlem Renaissance
        4) Jazz
    D. Women
        1) Appeals to female voters
        2) Flappers, birth control, and marriage
        3) Women in the workforce

E. Backlash
    1) Revival of the Klan
    2) Immigration restriction
        a) supporters of immigration restriction
        b) National Origins Act of 1924
        c) Mexican immigrants
    3) The Sacco and Vanzetti case
    4) The Scopes trial
        a) rise of Fundamentalism
        b) the trial
VII. The Hoover Peak
    A. The Election of 1928
        1) Herbert Hoover vs. Alfred E. Smith
        2) Analysis of results
    B. The "Great Engineer"
        1) Biography
        2) Political philosophy
    C. Bright Calm
        1) Hoover's agenda and achievements
        2) Economic danger signs

CHRONOLOGY

1914	Slav nationalist asassinates Archduke Ferdinand of Austria-Hungary.
1915	German submarine sinks the *Lusitania*.
	Ku Klux Klan reorganized in Georgia.
1916	General Pershing pursues Pancho Villa into Mexico.
	Wilson wins reelection.
1917	Zimmerman telegram.
	Congress declares war.
	Russian Revolution.
	Espionage Act passed.
1918	Daylight saving time introduced.
	Wilson advances his "Fourteen Points."
	Armistice in Europe.
	Spanish influenza kills thousands.
1919	Eighteenth Amendment ratified.
	Treaty of Versailles signed, but fails in Senate.
	Seattle general strike.
	Race riots in Chicago and other cities.

1919–20	Palmer raids.
1920	Congress passes the Volstead Act.
	Nineteenth Amendment ratified.
	Harding wins presidency.
	Nation's first radio station (KDKA in Pittsburgh) goes on the air.
	Sinclair Lewis publishes *Main Street.*
1921	Margaret Sanger founds the American Birth Control League.
1921–22	Washington Arms Limitation Conference.
1923	Harding dies in office; Coolidge becomes president.
1924	Teapot Dome scandal.
	Coolidge wins reelection.
	National Origins Act restricts immigration from Southern and Eastern Europe.
1925	F. Scott Fitzgerald publishes *The Great Gatsby.*
	Alain Locke publishes *The New Negro.*
	Scopes Monkey Trial.
1926	NBC established.
1927	Coolidge dispatches U.S. troops to Nicaragua.
	Advent of motion picture "talkies."
	Charles Lindbergh's solo flight across the Atlantic.
	Execution of Sacco and Vanzetti.
1928	Kellogg-Briand Pact outlaws war.
	Herbert Hoover defeats Al Smith for president.
1930	Smoot-Hawley tariff raises rates to historic highs.

ESSAY QUESTIONS

1. Why did the United States enter World War I on the side of the Allies, and how did the United States mobilize to fight the war?

2. Who in America benefited most from U.S. involvement in World War I? Who was hurt by it? You might consider the impact of the war on business, organized labor, farmers, women, blacks, immigrants, and radicals.

3. What were the sources of economic prosperity in the 1920s? Which segments of the economy lagged behind and why?

4. Describe the impact of science and technology on American culture and society in the 1920s. You might consider its effect on the economy, mass media, demographics, health care, the arts, and religion.

5. What were the key cultural divisions in America during the 1920s? How were they reflected in the election of 1928?

OBJECTIVE QUESTIONS

Multiple Choice

1. The outbreak of World War I was triggered by:
   a) the sinking of the *Lusitania*
   b) the assassination of Archduke Ferdinand of Austria-Hungary
   c) the torpedoing of the *Sussex*
   d) the Zimmerman telegram

2. Wilson ordered U.S. troops into Mexico in 1916 in pursuit of:
   a) Porfirio Diaz
   b) Francisco Madero
   c) Victoriano Huerta
   d) Pancho Villa

3. Between 1914 and 1917, U.S. public opinion turned against Germany because of all of the following except:
   a) U-boat attacks on Allied shipping
   b) British propaganda about alleged German atrocities
   c) the Zimmerman telegram
   d) Germany's support for the Bolshevik Revolution in Russia

4. To conserve food and materials needed for the war effort, federal administrators:
   a) introduced daylight saving time
   b) altered bicycle designs
   c) limited the production of alcoholic beverages
   d) all of the above

5. Bisbee, Arizona, was the site of:
   a) a race riot that left thirty-eight people dead
   b) labor unrest that ended when over a thousand miners were run out of town
   c) a bitter police strike
   d) an anarchist bombing that helped ignite the 1919 Red Scare

6. Wilson's framework for ending World War I, dubbed the "Fourteen Points," included all of the following except:
   a) self-determination for ethnic and national minorities
   b) freedom of the seas
   c) a League of Nations
   d) payment of reparations

7. World War I led to:
   a) the establishment of the German republic
   b) the liquidation of the Ottoman Empire

    c)   the creation of Czechoslovakia and Yugoslavia
    d)   all of the above

8. The Balfour Declaration:
    a)   pledged British assistance to the establishment of a Jewish "national home" in Palestine
    b)   gave parts of Germany to Belgium, Denmark, and Poland
    c)   established the League of Nations
    d)   formally normalized U.S. relations with Germany

9. During the election of 1920:
    a)   the Republican candidate promised to return the country to "normalcy"
    b)   a jailed candidate received 1 million votes
    c)   fewer than half of all qualified voters cast ballots
    d)   all of the above

10. The Kellogg-Briand Pact of 1928:
    a)   stopped all battleship construction for ten years
    b)   outlawed war
    c)   compensated Colombia for its loss of Panama
    d)   recognized Mexico's revolutionary government

11. Henry Ford revolutionized the automobile industry by:
    a)   introducing the assembly-line method of manufacturing
    b)   offering cars in a variety of colors and styles
    c)   allowing consumers to buy cars on credit
    d)   all of the above

12. During the 1920s, American farmers benefitted from:
    a)   rising prices
    b)   falling costs
    c)   the development of hybrid seed corn
    d)   widespread electrification

13. In *The Man Nobody Knows,* Bruce Barton:
    a)   portrayed Jesus Christ as a managerial genius
    b)   explored the shattering personal impact of World War I on a young American expatriate
    c)   critiqued hypocrisy and conformity in small-town America
    d)   indicted the anonymity and alienation of urban life

14. Marcus Garvey was:
    a)   a famous literary critic, known for his biting prose
    b)   a surrealist painter and photographer who drew inspiration from X-rays
    c)   a black Jamaican whose back-to-Africa movement attracted a large following among African Americans
    d)   a political anarchist who was convicted in the most socially charged criminal case of the 1920s

15. The National Origins Act of 1924 severely curtailed immigration from:
    a) England
    b) Italy
    c) Mexico
    d) all of the above

True or False

1. During World War I, the Central Powers consisted of Germany, Austria-Hungary, and France.

2. The Wilson administration paid the costs of U.S. involvement in World War I primarily through borrowing.

3. More U.S. troops died from Spanish influenza in 1918 than were killed in battle during World War I.

4. World War I contributed to a decline in union membership.

5. The United States recognized the new Soviet regime in Russia in 1920.

6. The "Palmer raids" targeted German Americans accused of espionage.

7. The nation's first radio station, KDKA in Pittsburgh, went on the air in 1920.

8. Taxes on the wealthy rose over the course of the 1920s.

9. "Welfare capitalism," used by companies to encourage worker loyalty, gave laborers a forum for wage and hour arbitration.

10. Clara Bow was the "it" girl of the 1920s.

11. After women were granted the vote in 1920, they frequently voted as a block.

12. The forerunner of Planned Parenthood was founded by Zora Neale Hurston in 1921.

13. During the 1920s, the Ku Klux Klan targetted Jews and Catholics as well as African Americans.

14. By 1930, most public high schools in the United States taught evolution.

15. In the 1928 presidential election, the Democratic candidate was hurt by his support for Prohibition.

SOURCES FOR FURTHER RESEARCH

Books

Ellen Chesler, *Woman of Valor: Margaret Sanger and the Birth Control Movement in America* (1992).

Lizabeth Cohen, *Making a New Deal: Industrial Workers in Chicago, 1919–1939* (1990).
Nancy Cott, *The Grounding of Modern Feminism* (1987).
Ruth Schwartz Cowan, *More Work for Mother: The Ironies of Household Technology from the Open Hearth to the Microwave* (1983).
Ann Douglas, *Terrible Honesty: Mongrel Manhattan in the 1920s* (1995).
Lynn Dumenil, *The Modern Temper: American Culture and Society in the 1920s* (1995).
James J. Flink, *The Car Culture* (1975).
Dana Frank, *Purchasing Power: Consumer Organizing, Gender, and the Seattle Labor Movement, 1919–1929* (1994).
Neal Gabler, *Winchell: Gossip, Power, and the Culture of Celebrity* (1994).
Martin Gilbert, *The First World War: A Complete History* (1994).
Maureen Greenwald, *Women, War, and Work: The Impact of World War I on Women Workers in the United States* (1980).
Ellis W. Hawley, *The Great War and the Search for a Modern Order: A History of the American People and Their Institutions, 1917–1933*, 2nd ed. (1992).
John Higham, *Strangers in the Land: Patterns of American Nativism, 1860–1925* (1955).
Kenneth T. Jackson, *Crabgrass Frontier: The Suburbanization of the United States* (1985).
David M. Kennedy, *Over Here: The First World War and American Society* (1980).
Thomas J. Knock, *To End All Wars: Woodrow Wilson and the Quest for a New World Order* (1992).
David Levering Lewis, *When Harlem Was in Vogue* (1981).
Frederick C. Luebke, *Bonds of Loyalty: German Americans and World War I* (1974).
Nancy MacLean, *Behind the Mask of Chivalry: The Making of the Second Ku Klux Klan* (1994).
Roland Marchand, *Advertising the American Dream: Making Way for Modernity, 1920–1940* (1985).
George M. Marsden, *Fundamentalism and American Culture: The Shaping of Twentieth Century Evangelicalism, 1870–1925* (1980).
Robert K. Murray, *The Politics of Normalcy: Governmental Theory and Practice in the Harding-Coolidge Era* (1973).
Susan Strasser, *Satisfaction Guaranteed: The Making of the American Mass Market* (1990).
Joe William Trotter Jr., ed., *The Great Migration in Historical Perspective: New Dimensions of Race, Class, and Gender* (1991).
William M. Tuttle Jr., *Race Riot: Chicago in the Red Summer of 1919* (1970).
Joan Hoff Wilson, *Herbert Hoover: Forgotten Progressive* (1975).
Neil A. Wynn, *From Progressivism to Prosperity: World War I and American Society* (1986).

Videos

The Great War: 1918 (58 minutes, PBS Video, 1990). Drawing on film clips as well as the letters and diaries of such fighting men as General John (Blackjack) Pershing, Sergeant Alvin York, and Sergeant Harry S. Truman, this documentary chronicles the story of U.S. soldiers in the closing battles of World War I. The program also features interviews with French and American army veterans and nurses who remember these battles.

The Great War and the Shaping of the 20th Century (8 hours, PBS Video, 1996). This eight-part series on the First World War begins with a sweeping look at the conditions that caused the cataclysm to unfold. Subsequent episodes trace the spread of the conflict across continents and peoples, explore the horrific nature of modern warfare, and discuss the myriad factors that ultimately led to Germany's collapse. The series shows how World War I produced "shell shock" in individual soldiers; mutiny in the French Army; the Russian Revolution; and the first genocide of the twentieth century, which targetted Armenians. In exploring the aftermath of the war and the failed peace, this documentary series shows how the "Great War" laid the groundwork for both World War II and the Cold War.

Influenza 1918 (60 minutes, PBS Video, 1998). Using archival photographs and film footage, this powerful documentary examines one of the nation's worst health crises: the 1918 flu epidemic, which ultimately killed half a million Americans and more than 20 million people worldwide.

Demon Rum (58 minutes, PBS Video, 1990). This documentary, originally shown as part of the series *The American Experience,* explores the impact of Prohibition on the city of Detroit, Michigan. Viewers meet the people involved in rum-running and operating speakeasies in the city. The film also discusses the enormous profits to be made in any illegal enterprise involving banned substances, and the eventual repeal of the Eighteenth Amendment.

New York: A Documentary Film: Episode Five, Cosmopolis, 1919–1931 (2 hours, PBS Video, 1999). The fifth episode of this series chronicling the history of New York focuses on the 1920s. The first hour shows how modern American culture was born, as the radio became available and jazz music poured out of Harlem. Many were attracted—and others appalled—by New York's glittery, fast-paced life. The second hour documents Al Smith's losing battle in the 1928 presidential election and the massive stock market crash of 1929. It also describes the city's skyscraper building spree, which ended with the dedication of the Empire State Building.

The Twenties (55 minutes, PBS Video, 1983). Originally produced for *A Walk Through the Twentieth Century with Bill Moyers,* this documentary highlights the contradictions of the decade. Usually seen as an age of speakeasies, flappers, and high living, the 1920s also saw millions of workers struggling for better wages.

Drawing on the reminiscences of Americans who lived through the period, this program explores the decade when old America was vanishing and a new urban nation was being formed.

Web Resources

"The Great War and the Shaping of the 20th Century," hosted by PBS, is the companion website to their video of the same name. Exploring the history and effects of World War I, it presents an interactive timeline, a gallery of maps and locations, interviews with nearly twenty historians of the war, an extensive bibliography, and links to related websites.

http://www.pbs.org/greatwar/

"The World War I Document Archive" offers treaties, official papers, personal reminiscences, images, and other primary documents assembled by volunteers from the World War I Military History List. Documents are organized by both subject (e.g., the maritime war, the medical front) and year. The site, which is hosted by Brigham Young University, also contains a World War I biographical dictionary, and links to other related sites.

http://www.lib.byu.edu/~rdh/wwi/

"Propaganda Postcards of the Great War," created by Paul Hageman and Jerry Kosanovich, reproduces war-themed postcards produced between 1914 and 1919 in four languages: English, French, German, and Dutch. During World War I, postcards were a major means of mass communication, and thus propaganda. The postcards available on this site all come from the extensive private collections of the two creators.

http://www.ww1-propaganda-cards.com/home.html

"Influenza 1918" features a timeline, maps showing the spread of the epidemic, snapshots of the disease's effect on three cities (Boston, San Francisco, and Philadelphia), and a discussion of Spanish influenza's symptoms and progression. The site, a companion to PBS's video of the same name, also offers a bibliography and interviews with experts about whether such an epidemic could happen again.

http://www.pbs.org/wgbh/amex/influenza/index.html

The National Archives offers visitors the chance to view "The Volstead Act and Related Prohibition Documents." Documents reproduced on the site include the amendments establishing and repealing Prohibition, a photograph of Detroit policemen inspecting equipment found in a clandestine underground brewery during Prohibition, and a memo pertaining to the investigation of a conspiracy to transport liquor during Prohibition.

http://www.nara.gov/education/cc/prohib.html

The Library of Congress's "American Memory" project offers "American Leaders Speak: Recordings from World War I and the 1920 Election." The site, which is searchable by keyword, subject, and speaker, presents fifty-nine sound recordings of speeches by American leaders made between 1918 and 1920. The recordings, which range from one to five minutes, capture the voices of Warren Harding, Calvin Coolidge, Franklin Roosevelt, Samuel Gompers, Henry Cabot Lodge, and General John Pershing, among others.

http://memory.loc.gov/ammem/nfhtml/nfhome.html

"Prosperity and Thrift: The Coolidge Era and the Consumer Economy, 1921–1929" assembles a wide array of Library of Congress source materials from the 1920s that document the widespread prosperity of the Coolidge years, the nation's transition to a mass consumer economy, and the role of government in this transition. The collection includes selections from personal and institutional papers; books, pamphlets, and legislative documents; excerpts from consumer and trade journals; photographs; short films and audio selections of Coolidge. The collection is particularly strong in advertising and mass-marketing materials.

http://memory.loc.gov/ammem/coolhtml/coolhome.html

"The 1920s," a site developed by Kevin Rayburn and hosted by the University of Louisville, offers a cornucopia of information on the cultural, political, and economic aspects of the decade. The site contains an extensive timeline; brief entries on subjects ranging from Prohibition to flagpole sitting, from the Broadway musical "Showboat" to the unveiling of Ford's Model A; and essays by Rayburn presenting contrasting views of the decade.

http://www.louisville.edu/~kprayb01/1920s.html

Extensive information on the Scopes Monkey Trial can be found on a website devoted to "Famous Trials in American History," developed by the University of Missouri–Kansas City Law School. The site includes Tennessee's anti-evolution statute; excerpts from the textbook used by Scopes and the Scopes trial transcript; observer's accounts; pictures, cartoons, and satire stemming from the trial; appellate court decisions; a bibliography; and related links.

http://www.law.umkc.edu/faculty/projects/ftrials/scopes/scopes.htm

"Herbert Hoover on the World Wide Web," hosted by the John Fitzgerald Kennedy Presidential Library, provides dozens of links to websites relating to Hoover and his times. Viewers will find links to the Herbert Hoover Presidential Library, to images of Hoover in the Library of Congress and elsewhere, and to audio clips and documents from Hoover's public life. The site also provides links to websites relating to the Roaring Twenties and the Great Depression.

http://www.cs.umb.edu/~rwhealan/jfk/hooverlinks.html

| The Great Depression and the
New Deal: 1929–1940

CHAPTER OBJECTIVES

- Understand the causes of the Great Depression, and assess its impact on various groups of Americans, including workers, farmers, and the middle class.
- Compare and contrast the political styles of Presidents Hoover and Roosevelt, as well as their approaches to dealing with the Depression.
- Characterize the New Deal, and explain how it evolved over time. Identify key pieces of New Deal legislation.
- Identify critics of the New Deal on the both the right and left, and discuss their arguments.
- Describe the impact of the election of 1936 on the nation's political landscape.
- Outline the reasons for the emergence and success of the CIO.
- Understand the role of the Supreme Court in the 1930s, as well as the motivation behind and fallout from President Roosevelt's "court-packing" scheme.
- Discuss the effect of the New Deal on workers, farmers, artists, African Americans, and regions like the South and West. Assess the legacy of the New Deal for the nation as a whole.

CHAPTER OUTLINE

I. Introduction: 1929
    A. Prosperity and Optimism
    B. The Stock Market Crash
II. The Great Depression
    A. The Economy in Free-Fall
    B. The Sources of Disaster
        1) Weak banking system
        2) Unequal distribution of wealth and income

       3) The timing of the downturn

       4) Economic orthodoxies

   C. Portraits in Gray

       1) Uneven impact

       2) The under- and unemployed

       3) Farmers

   D. The Dust Bowl

       1) Causes

       2) Consequences

   E. The Middle and Upper Classes

       1) Declining standard of living for many

       2) Taking advantage of the downturn

III. Herbert Hoover: The Engineer as President

   A. Response to the Depression

       1) Intervention by persuasion

       2) Embrace of an old orthodoxy

       3) Rejection of federal relief for the unemployed

   B. Declining Popularity

   C. The Bonus Army

   D. The Election of 1932

       1) Rejection of Hoover

       2) Rejection of Progressive approach to reform

IV. Franklin D. Roosevelt: The First Term

   A. FDR: The Politician

       1) Biography

       2) Political style and philosophy

       3) Personality and temperament

   B. The First Hundred Days

       1) Inaugural address

       2) Initial steps

          a) addressing the banking crisis

          b) Economy Act

          c) ending Prohibition

       3) Agricultural Adjustment Act (AAA)

       4) Tennessee Valley Authority (TVA)

       5) Banking regulations

          a) refinancing mortgages

          b) Federal Deposit Insurance Corporation (FDIC)

          c) Glass-Steagall Act

       6) Aiding the unemployed

          a) Civilian Conservation Corps (CCC)

          b) Federal Emergency Relief Administration (FERA)

       7) National Industrial Recovery Act

          a) provisions

           b) political compromise
      8) Ending the gold standard
  C. The First Two Years
      1) Assessing the First Hundred Days
           a) Agricultural Adjustment Act (AAA)
           b) National Recovery Administration (NRA)
      2) Growing criticism of the New Deal
           a) conservatives and the American Liberty League
           b) progressives
      3) Elections of 1934
           a) Democratic gains in Congress
           b) Upton Sinclair and End Poverty in California (EPIC)
  D. Stirrings on the Left
      1) Socialists
      2) Communists
      3) strikes of 1934
      4) Father Charles Coughlin
      5) Dr. Francis Townsend
      6) Huey Long
      7) public opinion shifts left
  E. The Second Hundred Days
      1) *Schechter Poultry v. the U.S.*
      2) Aid for the jobless
           a) inadequacy of early initiatives
           b) Works Projects Administration (WPA)
      3) Wagner Act
      4) Social Security Act
           a) unemployment insurance
           b) pensions for the elderly
           c) relief to mothers of dependent children
      5) Rural electrification
           a) Rural Electrification Administration
           b) major dam projects
  F. The Election of 1936
      1) FDR's campaign strategy
      2) FDR's landslide victory
      3) Reshaping the nation's political landscape
  G. Labor Rising
      1) The emergence of the Congress of Industrial Organizations (CIO)
           a) the limitations of craft unions
           b) John Lewis's vision
      2) Initial victory
           a) targeting General Motors
           b) the sit-down strike
           c) public sympathy

- 3) The movement spreads
        a) measures of success
        b) reasons for success
V. Roosevelt's Second Term
    A. Taking Aim at the Supreme Court
        1) The Court's threat to the New Deal
        2) FDR's Court-packing scheme
        3) Reaction
        4) The Court's shift
    B. The Ebbing of Reform
        1) Emergence of conservative opposition in Congress
        2) Southern Democrats and New Deal policies on race
        3) Midterm elections of 1938
        4) Economic downturn of 1937
        5) The Keynesian diagnosis
VI. The Social Fabric
    A. Demographics
        1) Declining birth rate
        2) Declining death rate
        3) Immigration slowdown
        4) Higher rates of education
    B. Cultural Trends
    C. Advances in Science and Technology
        1) Cyclotrons
        2) Commercial aviation
        3) Ground transportation
        4) Agriculture
VII. Muddling Through
    A. Achievements of the New Deal
        1) Role of the federal government
        2) New constituencies
        3) The social compact
    B. Limitations of the New Deal
        1) Race
        2) Distribution of economic power
    C. Charting a "Middle Course"

CHRONOLOGY

1929	Stock market crash.
1929–32	Herbert Hoover's presidency.
1930	Smoot-Hawley tariff enacted.

1932	Bonus Army clashes with federal troops.
	FDR defeats Hoover for president.
1932–45	Franklin Delano Roosevelt's presidency.
1932–39	Dust storms.
1933	Unemployment nearly reaches 25 percent.
	Agricultural Adjustment Act (AAA) passed.
	Tennessee Valley Authority (TVA) created.
	National Industrial Recovery Act (NIRA) passed.
	United States abandons gold standard.
1934	American Liberty League founded.
	Upton Sinclair campaigns for governor of California.
	Widespread labor unrest.
	Father Coughlin founds the National Union for Social Justice.
	Huey Long launches the Share Our Wealth movement.
1935	Huey Long assassinated.
	Schechter Poultry v. the U.S.
	Creation of the WPA.
	Passage of the Wagner Act.
	Passage of the Social Security Act.
	Rural Electrification Administration created.
	CIO founded.
	Appearance of Charlie Chaplin's *Modern Times*.
1936	FDR wins reelection in a landslide.
	CIO launches sit-down strike at GM.
1937	FDR proposes Court-packing scheme.
	Supreme Court upholds the Wagner Act.
	Renewed economic slump.
1938	John Steinbeck publishes *The Grapes of Wrath*.
	Antilynching bill fails in Congress.
	Fair Labor Standards Act passed.
	Republicans sweep midterm elections.

ESSAY QUESTIONS

1. What caused the Great Depression? Why was the downturn so steep, and why did it last for a decade?

2. Compare President Roosevelt's approach to economic calamity to that of Herbert Hoover and his Progressive predecessors. How and why did Roosevelt's approach change over time? Be sure to discuss specific actions taken by each president.

3. In your opinion, what were the three most important pieces of New Deal legislation? Why did you choose these three?

4. The Tennessee Valley Authority, the Rural Electrification Administration, and major New Deal dam projects brought the technologies of electricity, irrigation, and flood control to vast parts of the nation. What regions or groups benefited most from these programs? Who suffered as a result?

5. How and why did the election of 1936 reshape the American political landscape?

OBJECTIVE QUESTIONS

Multiple Choice

1. To Americans in the 1930s, "Black Tuesday" referred to:
    a) the stock market crash on October 29, 1929
    b) the advent of a particularly fierce dust storm in March of 1935
    c) a confrontation between police and Republic Steel workers in 1937 in which ten workers were killed
    d) the day the Supreme Court rendered its first ruling against New Deal legislation

2. At the height of the Depression in 1933, unemployment reached almost:
    a) 10 percent
    b) 17 percent
    c) 25 percent
    d) 40 percent

3. All of the following helped cause the Great Depression except:
    a) structural weakness in the banking system
    b) the unequal distribution of wealth and income
    c) widespread deficit spending
    d) protectionist measures, including high tariffs

4. Herbert Hoover responded to the Depression by:
    a) calling on business leaders not to cut wages or jobs
    b) lowering tariffs
    c) taking the United States off the gold standard
    d) all of the above

5. All of the following were passed during FDR's first hundred days except:
    a) Agricultural Adjustment Act
    b) Glass-Steagall Act
    c) Social Security Act
    d) National Industrial Recovery Act

6. The National Industrial Recovery Act:
   a) offered businesses relief from antitrust laws
   b) allowed government to step up regulation of business
   c) affirmed the right of workers to form unions
   d) all of the above

7. The American Liberty League was founded by:
   a) conservative businessmen
   b) progressive Democrats
   c) Upton Sinclair
   d) African Americans

8. "Share Our Wealth" was the slogan of a political organization founded by:
   a) the Socialist Party
   b) Father Charles Coughlin
   c) Dr. Francis Townsend
   d) Senator Huey Long

9. The WPA:
   a) reflected the assumption that unemployment was not going to quickly disappear
   b) paid more than relief, but less than prevailing local wages
   c) was criticized by both conservatives and labor unions
   d) all of the above

10. Labor unions' loyalty to the Democratic Party was solidified by:
    a) creation of the WPA
    b) the Wagner Act
    c) the Social Security Act
    d) the Rural Electrification Act

11. The first cabinet position ever held by a woman was:
    a) Secretary of the Treasury
    b) Secretary of the Interior
    c) Secretary of Labor
    d) Secretary of Agriculture

12. The election of 1936 was significant for all of the following reasons except:
    a) the Democrats replaced the Republicans as the dominant national party
    b) African Americans voted Democratic for the first time since Reconstruction
    c) the country saw a mass mobilization of new voters
    d) the third-party candidate garnered more than a million votes

13. John L. Lewis gained attention in the 1930s as:
    a) Secretary of Agriculture during FDR's first term
    b) the head of the Socialist Party

    c)   the founder of the CIO
    d)   a member of FDR's "black cabinet"

14. President Roosevelt's Court-packing scheme failed because:
    a)   the 1936 midterm elections gave Republicans control of Congress
    b)   the Supreme Court shifted and began upholding New Deal legislation
    c)   the Supreme Court ruled that FDR's plan was unconstitutional
    d)   all of the above

15. The Fair Labor Standards Act of 1938:
    a)   established a minimum wage
    b)   upheld the right of workers to engage in collective bargaining
    c)   contributed to the emergence of the CIO
    d)   all of the above

True or False

1. The stock market crash of 1929 triggered the Great Depression.

2. Some Americans made fortunes during the Great Depression.

3. Congress responded to the "Bonus Army" of unemployed World War I veterans by paying their promised bonuses early.

4. The Revenue Act of 1933 legalized the sale of beer and wine.

5. The Agricultural Adjustment Act paid farmers to limit their production of crops.

6. The Democratic candidate for governor of California in 1934 was a socialist.

7. During the 1930s, the Communist Party took the lead in promoting full equality for African Americans.

8. In *Schechter Poultry v. the U.S.,* the Supreme Court upheld the constitutionality of New Deal legislation.

9. The electrification of rural areas under the New Deal ultimately contributed to the exodus of farmers off the land.

10. The sit-down strike was first employed by the CIO in 1936.

11. With President Roosevelt's support, the first federal antilynching bill passed Congress in 1938.

12. The British economist John Maynard Keynes argued that the federal government should respond to high unemployment by balancing the budget.

13. High school and college enrollments rose during the 1930s.

14. The vast majority of books and films produced during the 1930s offered realistic depictions of social conditions.

15. The New Deal ended the Great Depression.

SOURCES FOR FURTHER RESEARCH

Books

William J. Barber, *From New-Era to New Deal: Herbert Hoover, the Economists, and American Economic Policy, 1921–1933* (1985).

Francisco E. Balderrama and Raymond Rodriguez, *Decade of Betrayal: Mexican Repatriation in the 1930s* (1995).

Michael A. Bernstein, *The Great Depression: Delayed Recovery and Economic Change in America, 1929–1939* (1987).

Alan Brinkley, *Voices of Protest: Huey Long, Father Coughlin and the Great Depression* (1983).

———, *The End of Reform: New Deal Liberalism in Recession and War* (1995).

Laura Browder, *Rousing the Nation: Radical Culture in Depression America* (1998).

Lizbeth Cohen, *Making a New Deal: Industrial Workers in Chicago, 1919–1939* (1990).

Blanche Weisen Cook, *Eleanor Roosevelt*, volumes one and two (1992 and 1999).

John Culver and John Hyde, *American Dreamer: The Life and Times of Henry A. Wallace* (2000).

Michael Denning, *The Cultural Front: The Laboring of American Culture in the Twentieth Century* (1996).

Lewis A. Erenberg, *Swingin' the Dream: Big Band Jazz and the Rebirth of American Culture* (1998).

Steve Fraser and Gary Gerstle, eds., *The Rise and Fall of the New Deal Order, 1930–1980* (1989).

James Goodman, *Stories of Scottsboro* (1994).

James M. Gregory, *American Exodus: The Dust Bowl Migration and Okie Culture in California* (1989).

Jonathan Harris, *Federal Art and National Culture: The Politics of Identity in New Deal America* (1995).

Robin D. G. Kelley, *Hammer and Hoe: Alabama Communists During the Great Depression* (1990).

David M. Kennedy, *Freedom From Fear: The American People in Depression and War, 1929–1945* (1999).

Ronald R. Kline, *Consumers in the Country: Technology and Social Change in Rural America* (2000).

William Leuchtenburg, *Franklin D. Roosevelt and the New Deal* (1963).

Jerre Gerlando Mangione, *The Dream and the Deal: The Federal Writers' Project, 1935–1943* (1996).

Robert McElvaine, *The Great Depression: America, 1929–1941* (1993).

Harvard Sitkoff, *A New Deal for Blacks: The Emergence of Civil Rights as a National Issue* (1978).

Bernard Sternsher, ed., *Hope Restored: How the New Deal Worked in Town and Country* (1999).

Studs Terkel, *Hard Times: An Oral History of the Great Depression* (1970).

T. H. Watkins, *Righteous Pilgrim: The Life and Times of Harold L. Ickes, 1874–1952* (1990).

Donald Worster, *Dust Bowl: The Southern Plains in the 1930s* (1979).

Videos

The Great Depression (7 hours, PBS Video, 1993). This seven-part documentary, produced by Blackside and distributed by PBS, traces America's greatest economic calamity from its onset in 1929 until its end a decade later. Various episodes highlight the impact of the Depression on laborers at the Ford Motor Company, iron and steel workers, tenant farmers, African Americans, and Okies fleeing the Dust Bowl. The series also documents the clash between federal troops and the Bonus Army, which helped cement President Hoover's downfall; President Roosevelt's landslide election in 1932; Upton Sinclair's run for governor of California in 1934; and the impact of the New Deal on cities like New York and the nation as a whole. The series ends with the 1939 World's Fairs in New York and San Francisco, and the start of World War II, which finally pulled the United States out of depression.

Surviving the Dust Bowl (60 minutes, PBS Video, 1998). Drawing on archival film footage, photographs, and interviews with witnesses, this documentary tells the moving story of those who endured America's worst ecological disaster. When the rains suddenly ceased in the summer of 1931, the ensuing black blizzards brought financial and emotional ruin to thousands of families in the southern plains.

Eleanor Roosevelt (150 minutes, PBS Home Video, 2000). For more than thirty years, Eleanor Roosevelt was at the center of this nation's history. Niece of one president, wife of another, and eventually U.S. representative to the United Nations, Roosevelt was, in the words of one biographer, "one of the best politicians of the twentieth century." Drawing on rare home movies and voice recordings, as well as interviews with her relatives, friends, and biographers, this documentary explores both the public and private life of one of the century's most influential women.

FDR (270 minutes, PBS Home Video, 1997). This four-part documentary traces the life of one of America's greatest presidents from his earliest political successes until his death in 1945. Among other things, it describes Roosevelt's bout with polio, his election to the presidency, his response to the Great Depression, and his leadership of the American people during World War II.

The New Deal Documentaries (105 minutes, Critics' Choice Video, 1995). These four government-sponsored educational shorts, originally produced between 1934 and 1940, are at once tributes to Depression-stricken America and examples of New Deal propaganda. *The River, The Plow That Broke the Plains, The New Frontier,* and *Power and the Land* were photographed by some of Hollywood's most notable cameramen. *The River* was also nominated for a Pulitzer Prize in poetry.

The Grapes of Wrath (129 minutes, produced by Twentieth Century Fox, released by Key Video, 1988). Directed by John Ford and starring Henry Fonda, this 1940 film classic is based on John Steinbeck's 1938 novel. It tells the story of the Joad family's migration to California from their dust-bowl farm in Oklahoma during the Great Depression.

Hoover Dam (56 minutes, PBS Video, 1999). Originally produced for *The American Experience* television series, this documentary tells the dramatic story of how an ambitious, hard-driving engineer turned a ragtag army of the unemployed into the nation's most celebrated workforce.

Scottsboro: An American Tragedy (90 minutes, PBS Video, 2001). The Scottsboro case was one of the most significant legal fights of the twentieth century. It began in March 1931, when two white women stepped off a box car in Alabama and alleged that they had been raped by nine black teenagers on the train. The trial of the falsely accused teens, recounted in this riveting documentary, drew the North and South into one of their sharpest conflicts since the Civil War, and helped spawn the modern civil rights movement.

Web Resources

"The Presidents," a website hosted by PBS, offers narrative, a bibliography, primary sources, and annotated web links related to Franklin Delano Roosevelt's early career and presidency. Among the primary sources included on the site are Roosevelt's inaugural addresses; his May 7, 1933, fireside chat; a 1935 message to Congress on Social Security; and a radio address to the CCC delivered the following year. The site also contains oral histories with various Americans about their experience during the Depression years.

http://www.pbs.org/wgbh/amex/presidents/indexjs.html

The "Franklin D. Roosevelt Library and Digital Archives," official website of the FDR Presidential Library, offers visitors access to thousands of digitized documents, photographs, and sound and video recordings, as well as links to other related sites.

http://www.fdrlibrary.marist.edu

"Voices from the Dust Bowl: The Charles L. Todd and Robert Sonkin Migrant Worker Collection, 1940–1941" documents the everyday life of residents of Farm Security Administration (FSA) migrant work camps in central California in 1940 and 1941. The searchable on-line collection, hosted by the Library of Congress's "American Memory" project, consists of audio recordings, photographs, publications, manuscript materials, and ephemera. It includes dance tunes, cowboy songs, traditional ballads, square dance and play party calls, camp council meetings, camp court proceedings, conversations, storytelling sessions, and personal narratives of the Dust Bowl refugees who inhabited the camps.

http://memory.loc.gov/ammem/afctshtml/tshome.html

"America from the Great Depression to World War II: Photographs of the FSA-OWI, 1935–1945" provides access to some of the most famous documentary photographs ever produced. The early images, taken by Farm Security Administration photographers, emphasize rural life and the negative impact of the Great Depression. This site, hosted by the Library of Congress's "American Memory" project, provides a searchable database and access to over 160,000 black-and-white images as well as 1,600 color photographs.

http://memory.loc.gov/ammem/fsowhome.html

Between 1936 and 1940, staffers at the WPA's Federal Writers' Project collected life histories from 10,000 Americans of various regions, occupations, and ethnic groups. People who told their stories included an Irish maid from Massachusetts, a woman who worked in a North Carolina textile mill, a Scandinavian iron worker, a Vermont farm wife, an African American worker in a Chicago meatpacking house, and a clerk in Macy's department store. Many of these documents are now available through "American Life Histories: Manuscripts from the Federal Writers' Project, 1936–1940," hosted by the Library of Congress. The histories typically describe the informant's family, education, income, occupation, political views, religious beliefs and mores, medical needs and diet.

http://lcweb2.loc.gov/ammem/wpaintro/wpahome.html

The Library of Congress reproduces more than 900 colorful and graphically diverse posters on "By the People, For the People: Posters from the WPA, 1936–1943." The posters were designed to publicize many projects of the Works Progress Administration, including health and safety programs, theatrical and musical performances, art exhibitions, and community activities in seventeen states and the District of Columbia.

http://memory.loc.gov/ammem/wpaposters/wpahome.html

"America in the 1930s," hosted by the American Studies Program at the University of Virginia, provides a window into the cultural expression of the decade. The site offers a wealth of materials organized into four categories: film; print; art, architecture, and design; and radio. Visitors can read articles on Harlem that appeared in the *Survey Graphic,* listen to early episodes of the radio show "Superman," watch film clips of the 1939 New York World's Fair, view slides of

Hoover Dam and the Chrysler Building, and watch snippets of various films produced during the 1930s. The site also contains a timeline, bibliographies, and
links to other on-line resources.

http://xroads.virginia.edu/g/1930s/HOME1/Default.htm

CHAPTER 25

Whirlpool of War: 1932–1941

CHAPTER OBJECTIVES

- Discuss the emerging threats to global peace posed by Germany, Italy, and Japan in the late 1930s, as well as the United States' initial response to these threats.
- Describe the sources of American isolationism in the 1930s and early 1940s, and show how this sentiment was reflected in specific U.S. policies.
- Explain how and why technology, particularly air power, reshaped America's thinking about its role in the world.
- Describe and explain the U.S. response to the refugee crisis in Europe between 1933 and 1941.
- Trace the international developments and changes in U.S. policy that eventually led to U.S. involvement in World War II.

CHAPTER OUTLINE

I. The Gathering Storm
   A. Adolf Hitler's Germany
   B. Benito Mussolini's Italy
   C. Japan's Imperial Ambitions
   D. American Isolationism
II. Encouraging Peace
   A. Roosevelt's Brand of Idealism
      1) FDR: the Wilsonian idealist
      2) FDR: the realist
   B. Trusting in Trade
      1) Trade agreements
      2) Recognition of the USSR

    C. The Good Neighbor Policy
        1) Commitment to nonintervention
        2) Liberalization of trade

III. Avoiding the Disagreeable
    A. Japanese Belligerence
        1) U.S. responses to Japanese aggression
            a) refusal to recognize Japanese control of Manchuria
            b) naval construction program
        2) Japan opens undeclared war on China
    B. Nazi Aggressions
        1) The Spanish Civil War
        2) Nazi eugenics
        3) Persecution of Jews
        4) Annexation of Austria
        5) The Munich Conference
    C. The Ingredients of Isolationism
        1) Isolationism's diverse constituency
        2) Widespread arguments favoring isolationism
            a) fear of military technologies
            b) claims of past mistakes: the shadow of World War I
    D. Legislating Neutrality
        1) The Neutrality Acts of 1935–1938
        2) The Abraham Lincoln Brigade
    E. The Refugee Question
        1) Refugee scholars and scientists enrich American life
        2) Many others kept out
    F. Defense for the Americas
        1) FDR argues for increased military preparedness
        2) The growth of air power
            a) aircraft carriers
            b) long-range land-based planes
        3) Only for the neighborhood
            a) airplanes for self-defense only
            b) from national security to hemispheric security
            c) isolationism continues strong

IV. A World at War
    A. The Outbreak of World War II
        1) The Nazi-Soviet pact
        2) Hitler's invasion of Poland triggers world war
        3) United States reaffirms its neutrality
        4) Germany's *Blitzkrieg* and the fall of France
        5) The Battle of Britain
    B. The American Response
        1) Pro-British sentiment

2) The mobilization of science
   a) concerns about the potential of uranium fission
   b) formation of the National Defense Research Committee
3) Making national defense a bipartisan issue
C. The Election of 1940
D. Battle in the Atlantic
1) U.S. responses
   a) destroyers-for-bases deal
   b) Selective Service Act
   c) lend-lease
2) Incipient Alliance
   a) Hitler's invasion of the Soviet Union
   b) the Atlantic Charter
   c) the *Greer* episode
   d) repeal of the neutrality acts
3) Passions and Power
   a) continuing isolationist sentiment
   b) Roosevelt's misuses of power
E. The Searing Japanese Sun
1) Japan's aggression in China and French Indochina
2) U.S. response
3) Attack on Pearl Harbor

CHRONOLOGY

1922	Benito Mussolini comes to power in Italy.
1931	Japanese forces invade Manchuria.
1933	Adolf Hitler is appointed chancellor of Germany. The Montevideo Conference.
1934–36	Nye hearings investigate the munitions industry.
1935	Mussolini sends Italian troops into Ethiopia. Spanish Civil War begins. Nazis issue Nuremberg laws. Neutrality Act of 1935.
1936	German *Wehrmacht* seizes the Rhineland. Neutrality Act of 1936.
1937	Japan opens undeclared war on China. FDR's "quarantine" speech. Neutrality Act of 1937.
1938	*Kristallnacht.* Hitler annexes Austria.

Allies appease Hitler at the Munich Conference.
Abraham Lincoln Brigade goes to Spain to fight for the
Loyalists.
Uranium fission is discovered in Berlin.

1939   Franco's fascists defeat Loyalists in Spanish-American War.
Hitler invades the rest of Czechoslovakia.
Nazi-Soviet non-aggression pact.
Hitler invades Poland, launching World War II.
Neutrality Act of 1939 allows sale of arms on "cash-and-carry" basis.

1940   Hitler invades Denmark, Norway, the Netherlands, Belgium, Luxemburg, and France.
The Battle of Britain.
FDR wins third presidential term.
FDR negotiates destroyers-for-bases swap with Britain.
Congress passes first peacetime conscription act.
America First Committee formed.
United States embargoes aviation-grade gasoline and metal scrap to Japan.
Japan joins Germany and Italy in the Tripartite Pact.

1941   Congress passes lend-lease bill.
Hitler invades the Soviet Union; United States makes USSR eligible for lend-lease.
Roosevelt and Churchill issue Atlantic Charter.
Roosevelt authorizes Navy escorts for British merchant shipping.
German U-boat attacks the *Greer.*
Congress repeals last vestiges of the Neutrality Acts.
Japan occupies French Indochina.
United States freezes Japanese assets in the United States.
Japan attacks U.S. fleet at Pearl Harbor.
United States declares war on Japan.
Germany and Italy declare war on the United States.

ESSAY QUESTIONS

1. What was the Good Neighbor policy, and how did it reflect the nation's foreign policy approach in the 1930s?

2. What were the sources of American isolationism in the 1930s? How was this sentiment embodied in specific legislative acts?

3. How did technology, and particularly air power, affect Americans' views about their nation's global role?

4. What steps did President Roosevelt take between 1935 and 1941 to defeat Hitler and restrain the Japanese? What events ultimately drew the United States into World War II?

5. How was the United States' entry into World War II similar to or different from its entry into World War I? (Review Chapter 23 if necessary.)

OBJECTIVE QUESTIONS

Multiple Choice

1. Japan invaded the Chinese province of Manchuria in:
   a) 1931
   b) 1933
   c) 1935
   d) 1936

2. The United States finally recognized the Soviet Union:
   a) because of pressure from American labor leaders
   b) in the hope that normalizing relations would lead to increased trade
   c) following the German invasion of the Soviet Union
   d) despite President Roosevelt's objections

3. As part of its Good Neighbor policy, the United States:
   a) adopted a policy of non-intervention in Latin America
   b) loaned destroyers to Britain
   c) sent the Abraham Lincoln Brigade to fight with the Loyalists in Spain
   d) pledged to defend the Philippines against a Japanese attack

4. The Nuremberg laws enacted by the Nazi government:
   a) called for the sterilization of epileptics, schizophrenics, and alcoholics
   b) abolished citizenship for German Jews
   c) barred Jews from attending theatres, concerts, high schools, and universities
   d) all of the above

5. At the Munich Conference, European leaders sought to appease Hitler by giving him:
   a) the Rhineland
   b) Austria
   c) part of Czechoslovakia
   d) western Poland

6. In the late 1930s, isolationists argued that:
   a) war would kill reform
   b) long-range bombers might destroy American cities

c) the United States had been lured into World War I under false pretenses
d) all of the above

7. Between 1935 and 1939, the United States tried to avoid involvement in another war by passing the:
   a) Neutrality Acts
   b) Atlantic Charter
   c) Lend-Lease Act
   d) all of the above

8. The Abraham Lincoln Brigade:
   a) sought to secretly evacuate Jewish refugees from Europe
   b) fought for the Loyalists in the Spanish Civil War
   c) was formed immediately after the fall of France
   d) worked to rally American support for China

9. The *St. Louis* was:
   a) an American gunboat that was sunk by Japanese planes while evacuating American officials from the Chinese city of Nanjing
   b) a ship carrying 900 Jewish refugees that was turned away from ports in Havana and Florida and eventually forced to return to Europe
   c) one of a new class of aircraft carriers, commissioned by the United States early in the Roosevelt Administration
   d) an American destroyer that was attacked by a German U-boat while escorting British merchant shipping

10. All of the following occurred in 1939 except:
    a) Franco's fascist forces defeated the Loyalists in the Spanish Civil War
    b) Germany and the Soviet Union signed a non-aggression pact
    c) Congress allowed the sale of U.S. arms to belligerents on a cash-and-carry basis
    d) German troops invaded France

11. The British turned back the Germans in the Battle of Britain largely because of the new technology of:
    a) radar
    b) long-range bombers
    c) submarines
    d) nuclear fission

12. FDR's opponent in the 1940 presidential campaign was:
    a) Wendell Willkie
    b) Henry Wallace
    c) Vannevar Bush
    d) Henry Stimson

13. The war and the New Deal hurt Roosevelt's support in the 1940 election among:

a) German-Americans
b) Irish-Americans
c) Midwesterners
d) all of the above

14. The America First Committee:
   a) called on the world to "quarantine" nations that spread violence
   b) investigated the munitions industry between 1934 and 1936
   c) argued that giving material aid to the Allies would keep the United States out of war
   d) insisted that American security would not be jeopardized by a Nazi victory

15. Before the Japanese attack on Pearl Harbor triggered war, the United States took all of the following actions except:
   a) embargoed the shipment of aviation-grade gasoline and scrap metal to Japan
   b) froze all Japanese assets in the United States
   c) broke off negotiations with the Japanese
   d) warned the Japanese that they would suffer dire consequences if they attacked British or Dutch possessions in Southeast Asia

True or False

1. Adolf Hitler broke the Versailles Treaty by sending his army into Ethiopia in 1935.

2. During the 1930s, Chinese communists and Chinese nationalists fought together against the Japanese.

3. The "cash-and-carry" provisions which the United States enacted in 1937 aided Britain and hurt Japan.

4. Between 1938 and 1941, the United States admitted fewer European refugees than were allowed under the restrictive immigration law of 1924.

5. By 1933, the United States had one of the most powerful armies in the world.

6. After the German invasion of Poland, most Americans believed the United States should go to war to save Britain and France from defeat.

7. "Chain Home" was an isolationist group in the United States that advocated keeping the U.S. military on a short tether.

8. In 1940, Democrats were more likely than Republicans to be in favor of intervening in World War II on the side of the British.

9. Uranium fission was first discovered experimentally in Britain.

10. President Roosevelt tried to build bipartisan support for national defense by naming Republicans to his cabinet.

11. The United States instituted its first peacetime conscription act in 1940.

12. The Atlantic Charter affirmed sovereignty and self-government as universal rights.

13. The famous aviation ace Charles Lindbergh argued passionately for U.S. intervention in World War II.

14. The *Reuben James* was an aircraft carrier sunk by the Japanese at Pearl Harbor.

15. The day after the Japanese attack on Pearl Harbor, the United States declared war on Japan, Germany, and Italy.

SOURCES FOR FURTHER RESEARCH

Books

Alan Brinkley, *The End of Reform: New Deal Liberalism in Recession and War* (1995).

Robert Buderi, *The Invention that Changed the World: How a Small Group of Radar Pioneers Won the Second World War and Launched a Technological Revolution* (1996).

Stephen Budiansky, *Battle of Wits: The Complete Story of Codebreaking in World War II* (2000).

Allan Bullock, *Hitler and Stalin: Parallel Lives* (1992).

Peter N. Caroll, *The Odyssey of the Abraham Lincoln Brigade: Americans in the Spanish Civil War* (1994).

Robert Dallek, *Franklin D. Roosevelt and American Foreign Policy, 1932–1945* (1995).

Irwin Gellman, *Good Neighbor Diplomacy* (1979).

Akira Iriye, *The Origins of WWII in Asia and the Pacific* (1987).

Manfred Jonas, *Isolationism in America, 1935–1941* (1966).

John Keegan, *The Second World War* (1989).

David M. Kennedy, *Freedom from Fear: The American People in Depression and War, 1929–1945* (1999).

Daniel J. Kevles, *The Physicists: The History of a Scientific Community in Modern America* (1995).

Deborah Lipstadt, *Beyond Belief: The American Press and the Coming of the Holocaust, 1938–1945* (1986).

Michael S. Sherry, *The Rise of American Air Power: The Creation of Armageddon* (1987).

Gerhard L. Weinberg, *A World at Arms: A Global History of World War II* (1994).

David Wyman, *The Abandonment of the Jews: America and the Holocaust, 1941–1945* (1984).

Videos

Lindbergh (58 minutes, PBS Video, 1990). A candid biography of the American hero and flying ace who became one of the nation's leading isolationists in the early years of World War II.

Charles Lindbergh: Against the Wind (50 minutes, A&E Biography Series). One of the greatest heroes in American history, Charles Lindbergh was later reviled as a Nazi sympathizer and anti-Semite. He flew into history when he piloted the *Spirit of Saint Louis* across the Atlantic, becoming the first to make the epic crossing. But his later advocacy of American isolationism during the period leading up to World War II made him a lightning rod for criticism. This documentary video draws on interviews with his daughter, friends, and historians.

Pearl Harbor: Surprise and Remembrance (88 minutes, PBS Video, 1991). Using newsreels, Hollywood movies, captured Japanese films, and other sources, this documentary looks back at the Japanese attack on Pearl Harbor and offers answers to questions that have haunted Americans ever since: Why were Hawaii and the United States so unprepared for the attack? Did FDR know the attack was coming, and why did so many ignore the warnings?

Pearl Harbor: A Documentary (180 minutes, PBS Video, 2001). Interviews with U.S. soldiers, Japanese aviators, and American civilians, as well as absorbing home movies, highlight this documentary about the unforgettable day the United States entered World War II.

World War II: The War Chronicles (490 minutes, International Video Entertainment, 1983). This seven-part series combines graphic combat footage and expert commentary to tell the military story of World War II from North Africa to Italy and from Pearl Harbor to Tokyo.

Prelude to War (65 minutes, PBS Video). This is the first in a compelling group of documentaries created and directed during World War II by master filmmaker Frank Capra in coordination with the U.S. War Department. The Oscar-winning series was created to help justify America's involvement in the war and to rally public support for the war effort. *Prelude to War* examines America's history, the nation's reaction to the terrifying events "across the ocean," and the change in its feelings from "America First" isolationism to involvement in the fight against the Axis.

The March of Time: War Breaks Out (660 minutes, PBS Video). For sixteen years, *The March of Time* newsreels were seen in over 50,000 theatres worldwide. This collection from the war years illustrates the many ways that Americans, from farmers to factory workers, prepared for war. The FBI geared up to combat sabotage in

America's defense industries, while panicky housewives hoarded foodstuffs under the threat of rationing. Powerful footage depicts the growing dangers in the Pacific and across the Atlantic, along with the increasing dominance of air power.

Web Resources

The University of San Diego offers a general guide to "World War II Links on the Internet."

http://history.acusd.edu/gen/ww2_links.html

"World War II Resources," created by Pearl Harbor History Associates, contains links to numerous primary sources that document the rise of tensions in Europe and Asia during the 1930s, the outbreak of World War II, and U.S. foreign policy in the interwar period. The site also contains more than 5,000 pages of original documents and testimony related to the investigations into the Japanese attack on Pearl Harbor.

http://www.ibiblio.org/pha/

The master lend-lease agreement, the text of the Atlantic Charter, U.S. declarations of war against the three Axis powers, and numerous other documents relating to the outbreak of World War II can be found at "World War II: Documents," hosted by the Avalon Project at Yale Law School.

http://www.yale.edu/lawweb/avalon/wwii/wwii.htm

Webcorp's Historic Audio Archives provides sound bites from the period, including British Prime Minister Neville Chamberlain's speech endorsing appeasement, Adolf Hitler's response, Winston Churchill's "Battle of Britain" speech, and President Roosevelt's "Day of Infamy" speech delivered after the Japanese attack on Pearl Harbor.

http://webcorp.com/sounds/

"America from the Great Depression to World War II: Photographs of the FSA-OWI, 1935–1945" provides access to some of the most famous documentary photographs ever produced. Taken by Farm Security Administration and Office of War Information photographers, the images show Americans in every part of the nation. In the early years, the project emphasized rural life and the negative impact of the Great Depression, but in later years, the photographers turned their attention to the mobilization effort for World War II. This site, hosted by the Library of Congress's "American Memory" project, provides a searchable database and access to over 160,000 black-and-white images as well as 1,600 color photographs.

http://memory.loc.gov/ammem/fsowhome.html

"America and the Holocaust," hosted by PBS, is the companion website to their video of the same name. Exploring the complex social and political factors that shaped America's reaction to the Holocaust, it presents narratives, maps, timelines, transcripts of interviews with program participants, original documents, and an extensive bibliography. Among the documents is a 1940 memo from a State Department official outlining effective ways to obstruct the granting of visas to Jewish and other refugees. The site also contains transcripts of letters that Jewish émigré Kurt Klein exchanged with his parents from July 1937, when he emigrated to the United States, until August 1942, when his parents were deported to Auschwitz. The letters document the older Kleins' constant struggle to join their children in America.

http://www.pbs.org/wgbh/amex/holocaust/filmmore/index.html

CHAPTER 26

Fighting for Freedom: 1942–1945

CHAPTER OBJECTIVES

- Outline the tensions within the Grand Alliance, the strategies used to win the war in Europe and the Pacific, and the key turning points in both military theaters.
- Describe the United States' economic and psychological mobilization for war, and the impact of that mobilization on the overall economy, labor, farmers, businesses, and various regions.
- Discuss the mobilization of science during the war, and the impact of both Allied and Axis technological advances on military strategy and the experiences of troops and civilians.
- Summarize the effects of the war on the home front, paying particular attention to the experiences of women, African Americans, Japanese Americans, and members of other minority groups.
- Explain U.S. responses to the Holocaust, and the impact of the war on domestic politics.

CHAPTER OUTLINE

I. Introduction
    A. Sources of American Strength
        1) Industrial production
        2) Ideology
    B. The "Grand Alliance"
II. Opening Gambits
    A. Strategy in Europe
        1) Anglo-American debate over strategy
        2) Operation Torch

        a)   the Darlan affair
        b)   German surrender in North Africa
  B. Demands in the Pacific
     1) Japanese advances in the Pacific
     2) The tide turns
        a)   Battle of the Coral Sea
        b)   Doolittle raid
        c)   Battle of Midway
     3) The battle of Guadalcanal
III. Mobilization and the Economy
  A. Production for War
     1) War Production Board orchestrates conversion
     2) Obtaining raw materials for war goods
        a)   curtailing civilian production
        b)   conservation
        c)   substitution
     3) Production miracles
  B. Controlling Prices
     1) Factors pushing prices up
        a)   soaring federal spending
        b)   wartime paychecks
     2) Paying for the war
        a)   income taxes
        b)   war bonds and other loans
     3) Office of Price Administration
        a)   freezes prices
        b)   extends rationing
     4) Controlling wage rates
        a)   National War Labor Board
        b)   Little Steel formula
     5) Office of War Mobilization
  C. Economic Boom
     1) Measures of the boom
     2) Labor
        a)   overtime pay
        b)   union membership soars
        c)   fringe benefits
        d)   wildcat strikes
     3) Farmers
        a)   soaring demand for farm goods
        b)   victory gardens
        c)   increased production
        d)   government price supports
        e)   agricultural income climbs

D. Regional Changes
  1) The South benefits
    a) military bases
    b) defense manufacturing contracts
  2) Wartime migration
    a) from farms and small towns to cities
    b) from region to region
  3) California

IV. The Enlistment of Science
  A. The Office of Scientific Research and Development (OSRD)
  B. Radar
    1) Advantages of microwave radar
    2) Alters Allies' offensive strategy
  C. A Physicists' War
    1) Proximity fuses
    2) Rockets
    3) Physicists' new status
  D. The Medical War
    1) Penicillin
    2) Fighting malaria
      a) synthetic quinine (Atabrine)
      b) DDT
    3) Blood
      a) freeze-dried plasma and albumin
      b) methods to preserve whole blood

V. The War in Europe
  A. Early 1943
    1) The Casablanca conference
    2) Anglo-American invasion of Sicily
    3) Tide turns on the eastern front
  B. Into Italy
    1) Political changes
      a) Mussolini resigns
      b) Badoglio regime surrenders
    2) Allied invasion of Italy
  C. Bombing Europe
    1) British and Americans bomb Germany
      a) British strategy
      b) American strategy
    2) Hitler bombs London
      a) V-1 rockets
      b) V-2 rockets
    3) United States turns to terror bombing
  D. The Invasion of France

        b)   Navajo Code Talkers
- 2) Mexican Americans
  - a) the *bracero* program
  - b) migration to war industries in Los Angeles
  - c) the "Sleepy Lagoon" trial
  - d) the Zoot Suit riots
  - e) volunteering for military service
  - f) changing attitudes of whites

VIII. Politics and the Limits of Freedom
- A. Japanese American Relocation
  - 1) The internment program
    - a) reasons
    - b) scope
    - c) Japanese American reactions
  - 2) Japanese Americans in the military
  - 3) Experience of other Asians
- B. The United States and the Holocaust
  - 1) Nazis launch the "final solution"
  - 2) Rescue movement faces obstacles
    - a) anti-Semitism
    - b) skepticism
  - 3) The War Refugee Board
    - a) successes
    - b) limits of the American response
- C. A Shifting Political Agenda
  - 1) Government policies aid largest corporations most
  - 2) Americans grow more conservative
  - 3) Congress begins dismantling the New Deal
  - 4) The G.I. Bill of Rights
- D. The 1944 Election
  - 1) Nominations
    - a) Republicans nominate Dewey
    - b) Democrats swap Wallace for Truman
  - 2) The campaign
  - 3) FDR's victory

IX. Victory in Europe
- A. Battle of the Bulge
  - 1) The German attack
  - 2) Eisenhower's strategy
- B. The Defeat of Germany
  - 1) Americans and Russians meet at the Elbe
  - 2) Liberating the concentration camps
  - 3) Hitler's suicide and Germany's surrender

CHRONOLOGY

1941   FDR's "Four Freedoms" speech.
Fair Employment Practices Committee established.

1942   Japanese occupy Manila.
United States interns Japanese Americans.
Doolittle raid.
OPA freezes prices.
Battle of the Coral Sea.
Battle of Midway.
Steel strike leads NWLB to impose Little Steel formula.
British and Americans launch bombing offensive against Germany.
Darlan affair.

1942–43   Operation Torch.
Battle of Guadalcanal.

1943   Casablanca Conference.
Germans lose battle of Stalingrad.
Congress repeals the Chinese Exclusion Act.
Wildcat strikes.
Detroit race riots.
"Zoot Suit" riots.
Mussolini resigns; Badoglio government surrenders.
Invasion of Italy.
Teheran Conference.

1944   War Refugee Board created.
Liberation of Rome.
Allies launch cross-channel invasion of Normandy.
Allies free Paris.
Hitler launches V-1 and V-2 rockets against London.
Battle of Saipan.
MacArthur returns to the Philippines.
Japanese launch kamikaze attacks.
Congress passes G.I. Bill of Rights.
FDR wins fourth term.
Gunnar Myrdal publishes *An American Dilemma.*

1944–45   Battle of the Bulge.

1945   Firebombing of Dresden.
Americans and Russians meet at the Elbe.
Germany surrenders.

ESSAY QUESTIONS

1. Churchill once said, "There is only one thing worse than fighting with allies, and that is fighting without them." What central strategic disagreements divided the United States, Britain, and the Soviet Union during the war, and how were they resolved? How did this affect the conduct of the war?

2. How did technological advances made by the United States, its allies, and its enemies, affect the waging and outcome of World War II? Support your answer with specific examples.

3. World War II has often been called "The Good War," both because of U.S. ideology and because of the social and economic impact of the war on various groups. Which groups benefited most from the war, and why? Who in American society might have disagreed with this description? You might consider, in particular, the experience of women, farmers, industrial workers, businessmen, and members of various ethnic and racial minority groups.

4. In 1943, President Roosevelt announced that "Dr. New Deal" had retired and been replaced by "Dr. Win the War." What did he mean by this, and what impact did it have on national policy? Considering the impact of the war in arenas ranging from economic policy to race relations, explain whether you think the goals of the New Deal were sacrificed to or furthered by the war effort? (Review Chapter 24 if necessary.)

5. How was the United States' experience during World War II similar to or different from its experience during World War I? (Review Chapter 23 if necessary.)

OBJECTIVE QUESTIONS

Multiple Choice

1. "I shall return." This famous comment was made by:
   a) General George C. Marshall
   b) General Douglas MacArthur
   c) Lieutenant Colonel James H. Doolittle
   d) Admiral Chester Nimitz

2. All of the following were resounding victories for the United States except:
   a) the Battle of the Coral Sea
   b) the Battle of Midway
   c) the Battle of Savo Island
   d) the Battle of Saipan

3. The United States met its wartime rubber requirements through all of the following measures except:

   a)   gasoline rationing
   b)   synthetic rubber production program
   c)   collecting used rubber goods from citizens
   d)   importing more rubber from Southeast Asia

4. During World War II, companies like Coca Cola and Wrigley Chewing Gum:
   a)   used the war emergency as an excuse to cut wages
   b)   garnered big federal subsidies
   c)   avoided sugar rationing by convincing military officials that soldiers and sailors craved their products
   d)   all of the above

5. The Little Steel formula:
   a)   set steel production quotas for plants in different regions of the country
   b)   shut down the civilian automobile industry so that steel could be diverted to the manufacture of tanks and aircraft
   c)   capped wages for the duration of the war
   d)   specified the amount of steel to be used in new battleships

6. Wartime migration boosted the population of all of the following except:
   a)   southern cities
   b)   Midwestern farms
   c)   Michigan
   d)   California

7. The technology most directly responsible for cutting Allied shipping losses in the North Atlantic in 1943 was:
   a)   microwave radar
   b)   the proximity fuze
   c)   hand-held rockets
   d)   the H2X radar

8. The disease which produced the most casualties among American troops during World War II was:
   a)   gonorrhea
   b)   malaria
   c)   typhoid
   d)   trench foot

9. During World War II, terror bombing was used:
   a)   by the British against Hamburg
   b)   by the Germans against London
   c)   by the Americans against Dresden
   d)   all of the above

10. "Seabees" were:
   a)   the flat-bottomed, diesel-powered craft used to land U.S. soldiers on invasion beaches throughout Europe and the Pacific

b) construction battalions who accompanied the Marines across the Pacific and who built U.S. military bases in the Pacific

c) groups of long-range and carrier-based American bombers that searched for German submarine wolfpacks in the mid-Atlantic

d) women who served in the Navy during the war

11. During World War II, the number of women who were employed outside the home rose by:
   a) 10 percent
   b) 33 percent
   c) 50 percent
   d) 100 percent

12. The "Double V" campaign was:
   a) African Americans' campaign against fascism abroad and racism at home
   b) the U.S. military's two-pronged strategy for victory in the Pacific
   c) the American and British pincer move that trapped German forces in North Africa
   d) organized labor's campaign to use the war to win fringe benefits for union members

13. During the "Zoot Suit" riots, American servicemen attacked:
   a) striking miners
   b) African Americans
   c) Mexican American youths
   a) Japanese American families

14. American responses to the Holocaust were limited because of:
   a) anti-Semitism
   b) skepticism that the Nazis were really engaged in a program of mass extermination
   c) fears that some rescue measures would aid the German military and hamper the Allied war effort
   d) all of the above

15. The nation's first political action committee (PAC) was formed in 1944 by:
   a) aircraft manufacturers, including Douglas and Lockheed
   b) the CIO
   c) the Congress on Racial Equality
   d) the American Jewish Committee

True or False

1. The United States won the Battle of Midway because of the numerical superiority of its naval task force.

2. Federal spending grew at a much faster rate during World War II than it had during the New Deal.

3. Between 1941 and 1945, the federal government kept taxes low to avoid disrupting the economy.

4. During World War II, two-thirds of all domestic military bases were located in the West.

5. The mass production of penicillin during World War II dramatically cut casualty rates among U.S. troops.

6. During World War II, blood plasma was segregated by race.

7. The Americans developed the first intermediate-range ballistic missiles in 1944.

8. The British bombing strategy initially focused on precision daylight bombing of specific industrial and transportation targets.

9. The Allied invasion of Normandy was code-named Operation Torch.

10. The Japanese military used kamikaze fighters throughout the war.

11. Most African Americans who left rural areas during the war headed to southern cities.

12. Members of the Hopi tribe gained fame as Code Talkers during the war.

13. In 1942, the United States shipped Japanese Americans living on the West Coast and Hawaii to inland relocation camps after several cases of sabotage were discovered on the West Coast.

14. The Battle of the Bulge, fought in the Ardennes forest in December 1944 and January 1945, was the bloodiest battle in U.S. history.

15. Seven times as many Americans fought in World War II as in World War I.

SOURCES FOR FURTHER RESEARCH

Books

Michael Adams, *The Best War Ever* (1994).
Karen Anderson, *Wartime Women: Sex Roles, Family Relations, and the Status of Women During World War II* (1981).
John Morton Blum, *V Was for Victory* (1976).
Nat Brandt, *Harlem at War: The Black Experience in WWII* (1996).
Alan Brinkley, *The End of Reform: New Deal Liberalism in Recession and War* (1995).

Robert Buderi, *The Invention that Changed the World: How a Small Group of Radar Pioneers Won the Second World War and Launched a Technological Revolution* (1996).

Robert Dallek, *Franklin D. Roosevelt and American Foreign Policy, 1932–1945* (1995).

John Dower, *War Without Mercy: Race and Power in the Pacific War* (1986).

Doris Kearns Goodwin, *No Ordinary Time: Franklin and Eleanor Roosevelt: The Home Front in World War II* (1994).

Gladys L. Hobby, *Penicillin Meeting the Challenge* (1985).

Maureen Honey, *Creating Rosie the Riveter: Class, Gender and Propaganda During World War II* (1984).

Akira Iriye, *Power and Culture: The Japanese-American War, 1941–1945* (1981).

John Keegan, *The Second World War* (1989).

David M. Kennedy, *Freedom From Fear: The American People in Depression and War, 1929–1945* (1999).

Daniel J. Kevles, *The Physicists: The History of a Scientific Community in Modern America* (1977, 1995).

Clayton Koppes and Gregory D. Black, *Hollywood Goes to War* (1987).

Nelson Lichtenstein, *Labor's War at Home: The CIO in World War II* (1982).

Gerald F. Lindeman, *The World Within War: America's Combat Experience in World War II* (1997).

Alice Yang Murray, ed., *What Did the Internment of Japanese Americans Mean?* (2000).

Gerald D. Nash, *The American West Transformed: The Impact of the Second World War* (1985).

William L. O'Neill, *A Democracy at War: America's Fight at Home and Abroad in World War II* (1993).

Bruce Schulman, *From Cotton Belt to Sun Belt: Federal Policy, Economic Development, and the Transformation of the South, 1938–1980* (1991).

Studs Terkel, *"The Good War:" An Oral History of World War II* (1984).

William M. Tuttle Jr., *"Daddy's Gone to War": The Second World War in the Lives of America's Children* (1995).

Harold Vatter, *The U.S. Economy in World War II* (1985).

Gerhard L. Weinberg, *A World at Arms: A Global History of World War II* (1994).

Videos

World War II: The War Chronicles (490 minutes, International Video Entertainment, 1983). This seven-part series combines graphic combat footage and expert commentary to tell the military story of World War II from North Africa to Italy and from Pearl Harbor to Tokyo.

The Men Who Sailed the Liberty Ships (60 minutes, PBS Video, 1998). Filmed on board the *Jeremiah O'Brien,* the last unaltered Liberty Ship still afloat, this film tells the tale of the 250,000 Americans who volunteered to sail cargo ships in World War II. These ordinary Americans performed one of the most dangerous jobs during the war. Civilians in war, merchant seamen faced every known hazard at sea and as a result, suffered one of the highest casualty rates of World War II. Often called the forgotten men of World War II, these remarkable civilian seamen volunteered to sail cargo ships in the face of overwhelming danger to stock the front lines of war.

The Battle of Midway (18 minutes, Barr Entertainment, 1991). A re-release of John Ford's famous motion picture, made for the Navy Department, depicting the Battle of Midway. Ford filmed the battle in color doing much of the camera work himself. During the action, Ford was seriously wounded. After his release from the hospital, he re-edited the film into its present form.

Home Front USA: 1941–1945 (390 minutes, PBS Video, 1990). A vivid and compelling series on life at home during World War II. Each man, woman, and child contributed in his or her own way: rationing; victory gardens, scrap drives, Red Cross work. By retooling its industry from peacetime to wartime production, the United States became the arsenal of democracy, as twenty-four hours a day, seven days a week, weapons and supplies poured out from America's factories to support the Allied forces. All these efforts and more are recalled in this multi-part documentary. Individual titles in the series include "America Goes to War," "Home Fires," "The Land of Plenty," "United We Win," "Arsenal of Democracy," "Rosie the Riveter," and "V for Victory."

Why We Fight (257 minutes, PBS Video). A fascinating and compelling group of wartime documentaries created and directed by master filmmaker Frank Capra (better known for *It's a Wonderful Life* and *Mr. Smith Goes to Washington*) in co-ordination with the U.S. War Department. The Oscar-winning series was created to help justify America's involvement in World War II and rally public support for the war effort. The seven documentaries are *Prelude to War, Divide and Conquer, The Battle for Russia, The Battle for Britain, The Nazis Strike, The Battle of China,* and *War Comes to America.*

The Life and Times of Rosie the Riveter (65 minutes, Direct Cinema, 1987). During World War II, women were called out of their homes to do "men's work" when there was an unprecedented demand for laborers. After the war, women wanted to remain in these jobs, but American society could not sustain such hopes. The story is told by five women—all former "Rosies"—who recall their histories in the workplace during this period.

"Free a Man to Fight!": Women Soldiers of World War II (52 minutes, Landmark Media, 1999). This documentary uses archival footage and interviews to tell the story of women who served in various capacities in all branches of the military: gunnery instructors, pilots, mechanics, code breakers, nurses, flight instructors, and others. These women reflect on their lives behind the lines, facing danger from without and often prejudice from within.

The Invisible Soldiers: Unheard Voices (60 minutes, PBS Video, 2000). This documentary looks at World War II through the eyes of the more than one million African American men and women in uniform. In interviews, they speak candidly of their accomplishments under conditions of racism. Veterans who tell their stories on the program include unsung D-day hero Waverly Woodson, who pulled drowning soldiers from the bloody waters; Edward Brooke, the first black U.S. senator in the twentieth century and a veteran of a key Italian campaign; and Senator Daniel Inouye, who owes his life to African American soldiers.

In Search of History: Navajo Code Talkers (50 minutes, A&E Television Networks, 1998). This documentary, originally broadcast on the History Channel, tells the story of the only unbroken code in modern military history: that created by Navajo soldiers during World War II. These soldiers wove their ancient language into a cipher that the enemies were unable to break. Numerous interviews with surviving code talkers illuminates their role, heroism, and motivations, and shows how their legacy affects the Navajo people today.

Without Due Process: Japanese Americans and World War II (52 minutes, New Dimension Media, 1992). During the war, race prejudice, war hysteria, and failure of political leadership resulted in the evacuation of Japanese Americans and their placement in internment camps in California, Utah, Arizona, Idaho, and Arkansas. This documentary highlights this violation of the Fifth Amendment, which insists on due process of law.

A Family Gathering (60 minutes, PBS Video, 1989). Focusing on the Yasui family, this documentary recounts the dramatic consequences of the United States' internment of Japanese Americans during World War II. The video, originally aired as part of *The American Experience* series, recounts the Yasui family's long battle to reclaim its place in American society.

The G.I. Bill: The Law That Changed America (60 minutes, PBS Video, 1997). The G.I. Bill guaranteed education, housing, and business loans to 15 million World War II veterans who otherwise would have returned from battle to dead-end jobs. In the process, it helped to create a vast new American middle class. Singer Harry Belafonte, writer Art Buchwald, Nobel laureate Martin Perl, NASA engineer Dan Herman, former senator Bob Dole, and others tell how this bill changed their lives.

Liberation (72 minutes, First Run/Icarus Films, 1995). Allied soldiers from Poland, Russia, Britain, and the United States recount their experiences liberating the concentration camps at the end of World War II.

Web Resources

The University of San Diego offers a general guide to "World War II Links on the Internet."

http://history.acusd.edu/gen/ww2_links.html

"World War II Resources," created by Pearl Harbor History Associates, contains links to original documents regarding many aspects of the war and postwar policy. Highlights include a series of studies of Japan's role in World War II, written by Japanese participants in the events at the request of the U.S. government; records relating to military intelligence and the U.S. campaign against U-Boats; the instruments of surrender for Italy, Germany, and Japan; and protocols and indictments for the German war crimes trials.

http://www.ibiblio.org/pha/

Numerous original sources relating to World War II, including German surrender documents, can be found at this website hosted by the Avalon Project at Yale Law School.

http://www.yale.edu/lawweb/avalon/wwii/wwii.htm

"America from the Great Depression to World War II: Photographs of the FSA-OWI, 1935–1945" provides access to some of the most famous documentary photographs ever produced. Taken by Farm Security Administration and Office of War Information photographers, the images show Americans in every part of the nation. In the early years, the project emphasized rural life and the negative impact of the Great Depression, but in later years, the photographers turned their attention to the mobilization effort for World War II. This site, hosted by the Library of Congress's "American Memory" project, provides a searchable database and access to over 160,000 black-and-white images as well as 1,600 color photographs.

http://memory.loc.gov/ammem/fsowhome.html

"America and the Holocaust" is the companion website to the PBS video of the same name. The site explores the complex social and political factors that shaped America's reaction to the Holocaust from "Kristallnacht" in 1938 through the liberation of the death camps in 1945. It presents narratives, maps, timelines, transcripts of interviews with program participants, and an extensive bibliography. The site also offers roughly thirty original sources, ranging from a lengthy visa application to newspaper reports to excerpts from government documents.

http://www.pbs.org/wgbh/amex/holocaust/filmmore/index.html

"Japanese American Internment Camps During World War II," hosted by the University of Utah, presents photographs and documents from the Tule Lake and Topaz internment camps. Tule Lake, in northern California, was one of the most infamous of the internment camps. Prisoners there held frequent demonstrations and strikes, demanding their rights under the U.S. Constitution. As a result, it was made a "segregation camp," and internees from other camps who had refused to take the loyalty oath or had caused disturbances were sent to Tule Lake. At its peak, Tule Lake held 18,789 internees. The internment camp at Topaz, Utah, was in the middle of an area charitably descibed as a "barren, sand-choked wasteland." At its peak, Topaz held 9,408 people in barracks of tar paper and wood.

http://www.lib.utah.edu/spc/photo/9066/9066.htm

The Smithsonian Institution's National Museum of American History presents "A More Perfect Union: Japanese Americans and the U.S. Constitution." Interactive galleries combine images, music, text, and first-person accounts, and allow viewers to share their own memories and responses. Visitors to the site are also able to search more than 800 artifacts related to the Japanese-American experience, including archival photography, publications, original manuscripts, artwork, and handmade objects.

> http://americanhistory.si.edu/perfectunion/non-flash/index.html

World War II posters helped to mobilize a nation. Inexpensive, accessible, and ever-present, the poster was an ideal agent for making war aims the personal mission of every citizen. The Smithsonian Institution's virtual exhibit "Produce for Victory: Posters on the American Home Front, 1941–1945" presents a selection of posters originally issued by government agencies, businesses, and private organizations.

> http://americanhistory.si.edu/victory/index.htm

CHAPTER 27

From Hot War to Cold War: 1945–1950

CHAPTER OBJECTIVES

- Describe the development of the atomic bomb, as well as the controversy surrounding its use on Japan.
- Discuss the origins of the Cold War, and trace the development and application of the U.S. policy of containment.
- Outline the domestic policies of the Truman administration from 1945 to 1950, discuss their political reception in Congress and elsewhere, and account for Truman's upset victory in the 1948 presidential election.
- Describe the impact of the Cold War on the U.S. economy, science and technology, and the struggle of minorities in American society.
- Explain the emergence of the Red Scare after World War II, and assess its impact on individuals and American society more generally.

CHAPTER OUTLINE

I. Introduction
   A. President Roosevelt's Death
   B. The Challenges Facing Harry Truman
II. Clouded Victory
   A. Roosevelt's Arrangements
      1) The postwar agendas of the Big Three
      2) The Teheran Conference
      3) The Bretton Woods Conference
      4) The Yalta Conference
         a) the key issues: Poland, Germany, Japan
         b) historical judgments about Yalta
      5) FDR's growing doubts about Stalin

    B. The War in the Pacific
        1) Savageness of the Pacific War
            a) propaganda
            b) blanket bombing of Japan
        2) Invasion of Iwo Jima and Okinawa
        3) Planning the invasion of Japan
    C. The Atomic Bomb
        1) The challenge of nuclear fission
        2) The Manhattan Project
    D. The End of the War
        1) The Potsdam Conference and Declaration
        2) The final hours
            a) bombing of Hiroshima
            b) Soviets declare war on Japan
            c) bombing of Nagasaki
            d) the Japanese surrender
    E. The Decision to Use the Bomb: Critics and Defenders
III. Entering the Peace
    A. America's Unmatched Power
    B. Worries, Foreign and Domestic
        1) Fears of recession
        2) Veterans' reentry problems
        3) Support for internationalism
        4) The creation of the U.N.
    C. The New President
        1) Biography
        2) Personal traits and beliefs
    D. Conservatism, Prices, and Strikes
        1) Congressional conservatism
        2) Price controls and inflation
        3) Widespread strikes
            a) UAW's strike against GM
            b) coal miners' strike
            c) railroad strike
    E. Political Earthquake: 1946
        1) Sweeping Republican victory
        2) The conservative Eightieth Congress
IV. The Emergence of the Cold War
    A. Debating the Origins of the Cold War
    B. Division over the Atom
        1) U.S. nuclear monopoly
        2) The Atomic Energy Commission
        3) Proposals for international accord founder
    C. The Doctrine of Containment

      1) George Kennan's brainchild
      2) The Truman Doctrine
      3) Critics of containment
  D. The Marshall Plan
      1) Reasons and scope
      2) Congressional reaction
  E. In Defense of Europe
      1) Stalin's actions in Eastern Europe
      2) The Berlin airlift
      3) Dividing Germany
      4) The creation of NATO
  F. The Far East
V. The Sinews of National Security
  A. The National Security Act
  B. The CIA
  C. Defense Research and Development
      1) Military support for research
         a) Office of Naval Research
         b) Atomic Energy Commission
      2) Jet-powered aircraft
      3) Electronic computers
VI. Prosperity and Tolerance
  A. A Flourishing Economy
      1) Baby boom signals optimism
      2) Reasons
         a) defense spending
         b) wartime savings and consumer demand
         c) G.I. Bill
  B. Faces Against the Window
      1) Continuing poverty
      2) Women in the workforce
  C. A Turn Against Intolerance
      1) Limits: Equal Rights Amendment fails
      2) Reasons for decline in intolerance
         a) wartime experience
         b) revelations about the Holocaust
         c) Cold War
         d) media attacks on prejudice
      3) Decline in anti-Semitism
  D. African American Aspirations
      1) Greater tolerance
         a) Jackie Robinson
         b) black musicians
         c) black workers and politicians

2) Continuing discrimination
   a) southern segregation
   b) federal housing policy
   c) armed services
3) African American protest
4) Supreme Court supports equal rights
   a) *Smith v. Allwright*
   b) *Morgan v. Virginia*
   c) *Shelley v. Kraemer*
5) Southern white resistance

VII. Truman Restored
  A. Politics and Minority Rights
    1) Truman's reelection strategy
    2) Support for civil rights
    3) Recognition of Israel
  B. The Election of 1948
    1) Democratic battle over civil rights
    2) Desegregation of the armed forces
    3) Defectors from the Democrats
      a) Dixiecrats
      b) Wallace's Progressive Party
    4) The Republicans
    5) Nature of the campaign
    6) Truman's upset victory
    7) Assessment
  C. The Fair Deal
    1) Congressional opposition
    2) Organized labor's strategy
  D. Medical Research
    1) Federally funded research
    2) Private support
  E. The "Fall" of China
    1) Mao's victory
    2) Debate over recognition
  F. Decision for a Hydrogen Bomb
    1) The Soviet atom bomb
    2) Debate over the H-bomb

VIII. Subversion and Security
  A. Fears of Internal Subversion
    1) International setbacks
    2) The Klaus Fuchs case
    3) Suspicion of communists and sympathizers
  B. The Truman Loyalty Program
    1) Reasons and scope

      2) Damage to civil liberties
- C. The House Un-American Activities Committee
    1) HUAC's makeup and agenda
    2) The Hollywood Ten
    3) Blacklisting
- D. The Case of Alger Hiss
- E. The Effects of Fear
    1) Conviction of American Communist Party leaders
    2) Loyalty oaths
    3) Chilling effect on culture and reform
    4) NSC-68

CHRONOLOGY

1943	Establishment of Los Alamos lab. Tehran conference.
1944	The Bretton Woods Conference. Supreme Court strikes down all-white primary in *Smith v. Allwright.*
1945	The Yalta Conference. Fire-bombing of Tokyo. Roosevelt dies; Harry Truman becomes president. Invasion of Okinawa. United Nations established. The Trinity test. Potsdam Conference and Potsdam Declaration. United States drops atomic bombs on Hiroshima and Nagasaki. Japanese surrender. First electronic computer (ENIAC) developed. Nuremberg Trials begin.
1946	Price controls ended. UAW, miners, and railroad workers strike. Churchill's "Iron Curtain" speech. George Kennan publishes "Mr. X" article. Strategic Air Command established. Atomic Energy Commission established. Republican Party wins control of Congress.
1947	Taft-Hartley Act passed. Truman issues Truman Doctrine and institutes Loyalty Program. National Security Act passed; establishes DOD, NSC, CIA. Brooklyn Dodgers sign Jackie Robinson. HUAC investigates Hollywood Ten.

1948	Communist coup in Czechoslovakia.
	Marshall Plan enacted.
	Berlin airlift.
	United States recognizes Israel.
	Executive order calls for desegregation in the military.
	Truman wins reelection.
1949	Creation of NATO.
	Creation of the Federal Republic of Germany.
	"Fall" of China.
	Soviets explode atomic bomb.
1950	Alger Hiss convicted of perjury.
	National Science Foundation established.
	Klaus Fuchs case.
	NSC-68.

ESSAY QUESTIONS

1. Why did the United States drop the atomic bomb on Hiroshima and Nagasaki? What are the principle arguments for and against this decision, and which do you find most convincing?

2. What caused the Cold War? What were the major sources of friction between the United States and the Soviet Union both during World War II and in the five years following the defeat of the Axis? How did each side respond to the actions of the other? Was one side primarily responsible for the worsening tensions or did both contribute?

3. What economic and social problems did the United States face at the end of World War II, and how did the Truman administration respond? Was the administration successful in pressing its domestic agenda?

4. How did the emerging Cold War affect the development of American science after World War II?

5. What were the causes and consequences of the postwar Red Scare?

OBJECTIVE QUESTIONS

Multiple Choice

1. The Western powers established the International Monetary Fund (IMF) at a 1944 conference at:
   a) Teheran

    b)   Bretton Woods

    c)   Yalta

    d)   Potsdam

2. The physicist in charge of the atomic bomb project at Los Alamos was:
   a)   Vannevar Bush
   b)   Enrico Fermi
   c)   J. Robert Oppenheimer
   d)   Edward Teller

3. The Potsdam Declaration:
   a)   warned Japan to surrender or suffer "prompt and utter destruction"
   b)   was issued by Truman after he learned of the success of the Trinity test
   c)   was promptly rejected by the Japanese
   d)   all of the above

4. At the end of World War II, the proportion of the world's gross annual product accounted for by the United States was roughly:
   a)   one-quarter
   b)   one-third
   c)   one-half
   d)   two-thirds

5. The permanent members of the U.N. Security Council include all of the following except:
   a)   Britain
   b)   the Soviet Union
   c)   France
   d)   Germany

6. The Full Employment Act of 1946:
   a)   strengthened unions
   b)   continued New Deal jobs programs
   c)   established the Council of Economic Advisers
   d)   all of the above

7. President Truman alienated many industrial workers in 1946 by:
   a)   extending price controls
   b)   asking for government power to draft strikers
   c)   signing the Taft-Hartley Act
   d)   all of the above

8. The doctrine of containment was first proposed by:
   a)   George Kennan
   b)   Dean Acheson
   c)   Harry Truman
   d)   George C. Marshall

9. The Soviets blockaded ground shipments to West Berlin in response to:
   a)   the announcement of the Truman Doctrine
   b)   passage of the Marshall Plan
   c)   plans by the United States, Britain, and France to form a West German state
   d)   the creation of NATO

10. The National Security Act of 1947 established all of the following except:
    a)   the Atomic Energy Commission
    b)   the Department of Defense
    c)   the National Security Council
    d)   the CIA

11. ENIAC was:
    a)   a South Pacific atoll that saw some of the most vicious fighting in the Pacific
    b)   the name of the plane that dropped the atomic bomb on Hiroshima
    c)   the first electronic computer
    d)   the call letters of the CIA-funded radio station that broadcast propaganda to Eastern Europe

12. America's postwar prosperity can be attributed to all of the following except:
    a)   a resurgence in defense spending
    b)   wartime savings and pent-up consumer demand
    c)   the G.I. Bill
    d)   deep tax cuts

13. As part of his 1948 reelection strategy, President Truman:
    a)   ordered the desegregation of the armed forces
    b)   recognized Israel
    c)   campaigned vigorously against the "do-nothing" Eightieth Congress
    d)   all of the above

14. In 1949 and 1950, a series of developments prompted U.S. officials to reevaluate their approach to Communism at home. These events included all of the following except:
    a)   the Soviet explosion of an atomic bomb
    b)   the "loss" of China to Mao's Communist forces
    c)   the Communist coup in Czechoslovakia
    e)   the Klaus Fuchs spy case

15. In 1947, the House Un-American Activities Committee (HUAC)   was catapulted back into the headlines after some years in obscurity with its investigation of:
    a)   spies in the State Department
    b)   communist influences in Hollywood

c) suspected subversives in the U.S. armed forces

d) faculty members who refused to sign a loyalty oath

True or False

1. The Big Three agreed to Germany's temporary division into four zones of occupation at the Potsdam conference in 1945.

2. More people were killed in the U.S. fire-bombing of Tokyo in March 1945 than died as a result of the atom bomb dropped on Nagasaki the following August.

3. The main technical challenge faced by the physicists responsible for developing a nuclear bomb was extracting or creating enough fissionable uranium and plutonium.

4. In accepting Japan's surrender, the United States agreed to allow the Japanese emperor to remain on his throne.

5. Roughly two-thirds of all American men between the ages of eighteen and thirty-four served in the armed forces during World War II.

6. At the end of World War II, most Americans agreed that the United States should once again withdraw from world affairs and focus on solving domestic problems.

7. The Marshall Plan was Secretary of State George C. Marshall's proposal to halt the spread of Communism by rearming Germany.

8. Most working women wanted to quit their jobs after World War II.

9. Revelations about the Holocaust contributed to the decline in ethnic, religious, and racial intolerance after World War II.

10. "Operation Dixie" was the postwar campaign by the Congress of Racial Equality to integrate interstate bus travel.

11. Former vice-president Henry Wallace led the Progressive Party challenge to Truman and the Democrats in 1948.

12. The United States' plan to stave off Communism by giving economic aid to Western Europe was called the "Fair Deal."

13. In the late 1940s and early 1950s, organized labor focused on winning cost-of-living increases and fringe benefits for workers.

14. The congressman who spearheaded the investigation of Alger Hiss's alleged espionage was John Rankin of Mississippi.

15. NSC-68 called on the United States to proceed to full-scale rearmament in order to meet the Soviet threat.

SOURCES FOR FURTHER RESEARCH

Books

Gar Alperovitz, *Atomic Diplomacy: Hiroshima and Potsdam* (1994).

————, *The Decision to Use the Atomic Bomb and the Architecture of an American Myth* (1995).

Barton Bernstein, ed. *Politics and Policies of the Truman Administration* (1970).

————, *The Atomic Bomb: The Critical Issues* (1976).

Paul Boyer, *By the Bomb's Early Light: American Thought and Culture at the Dawn of the Atomic Age* (1994).

Leonard Dinnerstein, *Antisemitism in America* (1994).

Richard M. Fried, *Nightmare in Red: The McCarthy Era in Perspective* (1990).

John Lewis Gaddis, *We Now Know: Rethinking Cold War History* (1997).

William S. Graebner, *The Age of Doubt: American Thought and Culture in the 1940s* (1991).

Alonzo L. Hamby, *Man of the People: A Life of Harry S. Truman* (1995).

Daniel J. Kevles, *The Physicists: The History of a Scientific Community in Modern America* (1995).

Walter LaFeber, *America, Russia, and the Cold War 1945–1996*, 8th ed. (1997).

Melvyn Leffler, *The Preponderance of Power, National Security, the Truman Administration, and the Cold War* (1992).

David McCullough, *Truman* (1992).

Richard Rhodes, *Dark Sun: The Making of the Hydrogen Bomb* (1995).

Ellen Schrecker, *Many Are the Crimes* (1998).

Allen Weinstein and Alexander Vassiliev, *The Haunted Wood: Soviet Espionage in America in the Stalin Era* (1999).

Stephen J. Whitfield, *The Culture of the Cold War* (1991).

Videos

The Day After Trinity: J. Robert Oppenheimer and the Atomic Bomb (88 minutes, Pyramid Films, 1980). A documentary on the life of J. Robert Oppenheimer, focusing on his role in the development of the atomic bomb during World War II.

The Atomic Cafe (86 minutes, First-Run Features, 1982). Compiled from propaganda films, newsreels, popular songs, and defense training films, this documentary offers a hilarious and chilling look at the hysteria surrounding the atomic bomb during the early years of the Cold War.

Truman (270 minutes, PBS Video, 1997). This documentary, part of *The American Experience* series, traces the life of America's most unlikely and least prepared president. Using news clips, photographs, and other documentary material, it follows his rise from a farmer to the man who decided to drop the atomic bomb on Japan and who confronted the expanding Soviet threat.

Cold War (20 hours, PBS Video, 1998). This twenty-four-part documentary, originally produced for CNN, uses newly released footage to tell the story of the Cold War, giving particular attention to the years from 1945 to 1960. Episodes take the viewer inside the Pentagon, the Kremlin, and the missile sites in Cuba, to Yalta and Potsdam, Budapest and Berlin, and Hanoi and Panmunjon.

The Berlin Airlift (60 minutes, PBS Video). On June 24, 1948, the Soviet Union imposed a blockade on the western sectors of Berlin. Overnight, two and a half million Berliners were cut off from food and fuel and surrounded by a sea of 300,000 Soviet troops. Using archival film, home movies, and interviews with those who lived through it, this documentary looks at the twentieth century's most dramatic humanitarian rescue effort, the story of the British and American troops who flew 277,000 trips to deliver more than two million tons of food and supplies to keep Berlin's inhabitants alive.

Boomtime, 1948 (60 minutes, PBS Video, 1999). After World War II, the United States enjoyed unparalleled prosperity while Europe and much of the rest of the world suffered from devastation, lack of food and other necessities, and unemployment. As this documentary shows, the Marshall Plan assisted Europe greatly in its recovery from the war and helped Europeans learn the "American way" of doing things. Europeans began changing their economy by themselves and became consumers as well as producers. This prosperity lasted until 1973, when the certainty of cheap oil and a world dominated by the West was over.

The G.I. Bill: The Law That Changed America (60 minutes, PBS Video, 1997). The G.I. Bill guaranteed education, housing, and business loans to 15 million World War II veterans who otherwise would have returned from battle to dead-end jobs. In the process, it helped to create a vast new American middle class. Singer Harry Belafonte, writer Art Buchwald, Nobel laureate Martin Perl, NASA engineer Dan Herman, former senator Bob Dole, and others tell how this bill changed their lives.

Race for the Superbomb (120 minutes, PBS Video, 1999). This documentary, originally aired as part of *The American Experience,* draws on civil defense films, recently declassified military footage, and newly discovered Soviet archival sources to tell the spellbinding story of the race to build the hydrogen bomb. Physicist Edward Teller defends the bomb as a deterrent to a Soviet attack, while physicists Robert Oppenheimer and Enrico Fermi see it as nothing less than a monster of mass destruction. Meanwhile, Americans everywhere prepare for what they expect to be a terrifying war.

Seeing Red, Stories of American Communists (100 minutes, Facets Video, 1984). Drawing on over 400 interviews with present and former American Communists, this video paints an engaging portrait of American Communism from its heyday in the 1930s through the bitter McCarthy-era witchhunts of the 1950s. This film won an Academy Award nomination for Best Feature Documentary.

Web Resources

Documents relating to the wartime conferences of the Big Three, including the agreements reached at Yalta and Potsdam, can be found at "World War II: Documents," hosted by the Avalon Project at Yale Law School.

http://www.yale.edu/lawweb/avalon/wwii/wwii.htm

"World War II Resources," a website created by Pearl Harbor History Associates, contains a series of studies of Japan's role in World War II, written by Japanese participants in the events at the request of the U.S. government; the instruments of surrender for Japan; and an article on the U.S. plan to invade Japan and the Japanese plan to resist that invasion.

http://www.ibiblio.org/pha/

"The Presidents," a website hosted by PBS, offers both narrative and primary sources related to Harry S. Truman's early career, domestic and foreign policy, and legacy. Documents include Truman's 1947 address to the NAACP, his 1948 executive order desegregating the armed forces, and his 1949 inaugural address.

http://www.pbs.org/wgbh/amex/presidents/indexjs.html

More than twenty original documents detailing the U.S. decision to drop the atomic bomb on Hiroshima and Nagasaki are presented on the website "Atomic Bomb: Decision." The documents, most of which come from the National Archives, include the minutes of various scientific committees, eyewitness accounts of the Trinity test, and excerpts from President Truman's diary.

http://www.dannen.com/decision/index.html

CHAPTER 28 | Korea, Eisenhower, and Affluence: 1950–1956

CHAPTER OBJECTIVES

- Discuss the impact of the Korean War on American society, including its effect on scientific research and development, domestic anti-Communism, the economy, and U.S. foreign policy.
- Describe Eisenhower's political philosophy and style, as well as his major domestic accomplishments and failures.
- Understand Eisenhower's approach to national security with regard to both the Soviet Union and the Third World, and outline the key foreign policy decisions he faced.
- Describe the impact of both prosperity and the Cold War on the lifestyles of middle-class, white Americans in the late 1950s, and identify those left behind by the culture of affluence.
- Account for the resurgence of civil rights activism in the mid-to-late 1950s.

CHAPTER OUTLINE

I. Introduction
   A. The Outbreak of the Korean War
   B. Scope of the U.S. Commitment
II. Korea and Its Consequences
   A. A Seesaw War
      1) MacArthur's assault on Inchon
      2) Crossing the 38th parallel
      3) Chinese intervention
   B. The Sacking of MacArthur
      1) MacArthur's insubordination and removal
      2) Stalled peace negotiations

    C. Extending Containment
- 1) Changing views
  - a) the Sino-Soviet bloc
  - b) the Communist threat as military and global
- 2) Implementation

    D. A Sea Change in Defense Science
- 1) Intensified support for military technology
- 2) Development of the hydrogen bomb

    E. McCarthyism
- 1) Senator McCarthy's rise and methods
- 2) His supporters
- 3) The intensifying Red Scare

III. They Liked Ike

    A. The Election of 1952
- 1) GOP nominee: Dwight Eisenhower
- 2) Democratic nominee: Adlai Stevenson
- 3) Nixon's "Checkers" speech
- 4) Eisenhower's television ads
- 5) Republican victory

    B. Eisenhower the Centrist
- 1) Biography and style
- 2) Approach to foreign policy

    C. Ending the Korean War
- 1) Terms of the cease-fire
- 2) Casualties and other costs

    D. Dealing with McCarthyism
- 1) Eisenhower's anti-Communism
- 2) Red-baiting Oppenheimer
- 3) The Army-McCarthy hearings
- 4) McCarthy's censure

    E. Accommodating to the Welfare State
- 1) Eisenhower's philosophy on domestic affairs
- 2) Environmental policy
- 3) Preserving the New Deal/Fair Deal

    F. The Election of 1956

IV. Eisenhower and the World

    A. The "New Look": Massive Retaliation

    B. Rockets and Missiles
- 1) Strategic nuclear weapons
- 2) Tactical nuclear weapons

    C. Staying Ahead of the Soviets
- 1) U-2 flights
- 2) Minuteman missiles
- 3) Submarine-based missiles

D. Arms Control Initiatives
   1) "Atoms for Peace"
   2) "Open Skies"
E. Demand for a Test Ban
   1) The *Lucky Dragon* incident
   2) Growing fears about health risks
   3) Calls for a limited test ban
V. Superpower Shift
A. A Shifting Focus
   1) The Hungarian revolution
   2) Vying for the Third World
B. Securing the Third World: The CIA
   1) The Philippines
   2) Iran
   3) Guatemala
C. The Suez Crisis and the Middle East
   1) The Suez crisis
   2) The Eisenhower Doctrine
D. Worries over Indochina
   1) The Vietminh's struggle against the French
   2) Eisenhower's "Domino Theory"
   3) Subverting the Geneva accords
E. Security in Southeast Asia
   1) Formation of SEATO
   2) The Formosa Resolution
VI. The Cold War, Technology, and the Economy
A. "Military Keynsianism"
   1) Scope of defense expenditures
   2) Impact on the South and West
   3) The interstate highway system
B. Defense and Technical Competitiveness
C. Civilian Spinoffs
   1) Impact on various industries
   2) Development of the transistor
D. Computers
   1) High-speed digital computers
   2) Real-time computers
   3) Magnetic core memory
   4) IBM
E. Agriculture
   1) Farm technologies and federal policy
   2) The trend towards agribusiness
   3) Impact on southern agriculture
VII. "The Golden Age Is Now"

    A. 1950s Prosperity: Reasons and Measures
    B. Health
        1) Prescription drugs
        2) Vanquishing polio
    C. Labor
        1) Improved benefits and working conditions
        2) Decline in union militancy
        3) Diminishing power of unions
    D. Women and Work
        1) Cultural messages against women working
        2) The embrace of domesticity
        3) Growing discontent
        4) Women in the workforce
VIII. Migrations and the Melting Pot
    A. Migration to the Sunbelt
    B. The Flight from Downtown
        1) Cheap suburban housing
        2) Federal housing and tax policy
        3) The impact on cities
    C. Suburbia and Assimilation
    D. Asian Americans
        1) Changes in immigration law
        2) Continuing discrimination
        3) Generational conflict
    E. The Revival of Religion
        1) Reasons for revival
            a) churches as social centers
            b) television and mass mailings
        2) Tone of revival
        3) Religion and anti-Communism
IX. Outcasts of Affluence
    A. Continuing Poverty
    B. Hispanic Americans
        1) Puerto Ricans
        2) Mexican Americans
    C. Native Americans
        1) State voting rights
        2) "Termination" and "relocation"
    D. African Americans
        1) Racial integration of the armed forces
        2) Migration from the South
        3) Housing discrimination in the North
        4) Job discrimination in the North
X. Stirrings for Civil Rights

A. Factors Encouraging Protest
   1) End of McCarthyism
   2) Returning black veterans
   3) Television
   4) Growing black urban middle class
B. *Brown v. Board of Education*
C. The Montgomery Bus Boycott
D. White Resistance
   1) Southern resistance to school integration
   2) Antiblack violence
   3) Founding of the SCLC
   4) Growing white support for civil rights
   5) Eisenhower's views

CHRONOLOGY

1946	Dr. Spock's *Common Sense Book of Baby and Child Care* published.
1948	Bell Telephone Labs develops the transistor. Levittown opens on Long Island.
1950	McCarthy's Wheeling, West Virginia, speech. Internal Security Act. Diner's Club introduces the credit card.
1950–53	The Korean War.
1951	Truman sacks MacArthur.
1952	First U.S. H-bomb test. McCarran-Walter Act. Publication of Ralph Ellison's *The Invisible Man*.
1953–60	Dwight Eisenhower's presidency.
1953	Execution of Julius and Ethel Rosenberg. Stalin's death. CIA aids Iranian coup.
1954	Dulles announces Eisenhower's "New Look" strategy. The Suez Crisis. French garrison at Dien Bien Phu surrenders. Geneva peace conference. Congress adds "Under God" to Pledge of Allegiance. Supreme Court rules in *Brown v. Board of Education*. Army-McCarthy Hearings.

1955	United States begins U-2 surveillance flights.
	Khruschev rejects DDE's "Open Skies" initiative.
	AFL and CIO merge.
	Emmett Till's murder.
1955–56	Montgomery Bus Boycott.
1956	Eisenhower wins reelection.
	Hungarian uprising.
	Interstate Highway Act.
1957	Formation of the Southern Christian Leadership Conference (SCLC).
1958	Test ban talks begin in Geneva.

ESSAY QUESTIONS

1. How did the Korean War affect American society and politics both at home and abroad? Consider, in particular, the war's impact on the economy, scientific research and development, domestic anti-Communism, and the doctrine of containment.

2. What were the chief components of Eisenhower's approach to foreign policy, and how did he justify them? How were they similar to or different from those of his predecessor?

3. What were the Eisenhower administration's chief domestic accomplishments?

4. "While history textbooks often emphasize immigration *to* America, Americans' internal migrations during and after World War II—the migration of African Americans to the urban North, and of diverse Americans to the Sunbelt and suburbs—had an equally profound impact on American life." Comment critically on this statement, supporting your answer with specific examples.

5. What factors accounted for the surge in civil rights activism in the mid-1950s? What form did that activism take, and what resistance did it encounter?

OBJECTIVE QUESTIONS

Multiple Choice

1. China warned that it would intervene in the Korean War if U.S. troops approached:
   a) the 38th parallel

b) the Yalu River
c) the Inchon peninsula
d) Pusan

2. Peace negotiations to end the Korean War bogged down over the issue of:
   a) the borders of North and South Korea
   b) the repatriation of North Korean and Chinese prisoners
   c) the permanent removal of U.S. troops
   d) a place for China on the U.N. Security Council

3. The Korean War:
   a) encouraged U.S. policymakers to see the Soviet Union and Communist China as a monolithic bloc
   b) prompted the United States to rearm Germany
   c) contributed to the rapid development of the hydrogen bomb
   d) all of the above

4. Dwight Eisenhower's running mate in the 1952 presidential election was:
   a) Robert Taft
   b) Adlai Stevenson
   c) Richard Nixon
   d) John Foster Dulles

5. Dwight Eisenhower:
   a) intentionally muddled his syntax to confuse reporters and critics
   b) worked to dismantle the New Deal/Fair Deal
   c) threw the weight of the federal government behind efforts to desegregate the South
   d) all of the above

6. All of the following were missiles developed by the United States during the 1950s except:
   a) the Atlas
   b) the U-2
   c) the Minuteman
   d) the Polaris

7. *Lucky Dragon* was:
   a) a Japanese fishing boat caught in the fallout of an American H-bomb test
   b) a science fiction movie about genetic mutations triggered by nuclear radiation
   c) the code name for a U.S. plan to protect Formosa from mainland China
   d) a movie about generational conflict set in San Francisco's Chinatown

8. The Eisenhower Doctrine:
   a) committed the United States to send military aid to any nation in the Middle East that felt itself threatened by "international communism"

b) urged stimulation of the economy by military spending

c) gave the president blanket authority to use military forces to protect Taiwan

d) called for extensive use of the CIA to shore up anti-Communist regimes in the Third World

9. Eisenhower first articulated the "domino theory" in connection with events in:

a) Egypt

b) Vietnam

c) Iran

d) Taiwan

10. The average life span of Americans rose dramatically between 1940 and 1960, primarily because of:

a) improvements in the American diet

b) the development of antibiotics and other drugs

c) a new enthusiasm for fitness and exercise

d) reductions in the use of DDT and other cancer-causing chemicals

11. The power of unions declined in the late 1950s in part because of:

a) internal divisions among the unions' many immigrant members

b) violent strike-breaking techniques used by many corporations

c) the growing number of public employees and white-collar workers

d) all of the above

12. The state that benefited most from Americans' postwar migration was:

a) New York

b) Florida

c) California

d) Illinois

13. Americans' move to the suburbs after World War II was driven by all of the following except:

a) the G.I. Bill

b) federal tax policy

c) urban renewal programs

d) federally funded highway construction

14. In the 1950s, Americans flocked to churches and synagogues in record numbers, reflecting:

a) the desire of many Americans to overcome isolation and create a sense of community in the new world of the suburbs.

b) evangelists' new reliance on mass mailings and television

c) the influence of the Cold War, which cast atheism as un-American

d) all of the above

15. All of the following developments helped fuel the southern civil rights movement except:
    a) the integration of the armed services
    b) the growth of the black urban middle class
    c) a decline in racial violence in the South
    d) the U.S. desire to win Cold War allies in the Third World

True or False

1. President Truman sacked General MacArthur for failing to push the Chinese back to the Yalu River.

2. A cocker spaniel named "Checkers" helped save vice-presidential nominee Richard Nixon's spot on the Republican ticket.

3. The Korean War ended in a clear victory for the United States.

4. After the Korean War, some 50,000 Chinese and North Korean prisoners of war chose not to return to their countries.

5. J. Robert Oppenheimer, the physicist who headed America's wartime effort to develop the atomic bomb, was ruled a "security risk" in 1954.

6. Senator Joseph McCarthy was ultimately brought down by his attack on the U.S. Army.

7. After World War II, the American military brought Nazi rocket scientists to the United States to help develop its missile program.

8. Eisenhower's national security policy relied on "massive retaliation" despite the fact that nuclear weapons were much more expensive than a conventionally equipped army.

9. Between 1954 and 1960, nearly half the federal budget was spent on defense.

10. American Express introduced the first credit card in 1950.

11. American prosperity during the 1950s can be attributed in part to sharp cutbacks in federal social programs like Social Security.

12. Dr. Benjamin Spock is best known for developing an effective vaccine against polio.

13. The percentage of women between eighteen and twenty-four who were married fell dramatically between 1940 and 1950.

14. The Eisenhower administration's termination program successfully helped most Native Americans assimilate into white society.

15. African Americans who migrated north settled in central cities in part because federal lending policies made it difficult for them to buy suburban homes.

SOURCES FOR FURTHER RESEARCH

Books

Stephen Ambrose, *Eisenhower,* 2 vols. (1984).
Clay Blair, *The Forgotten War: America in Korea 1950–1953* (1987).
Taylor Branch, *Parting the Waters: America in the King Years, 1954–1963* (1988).
Bruce Cumings, *The Origins of the Korean War*, 2 vols. (1981–1990).
Mary L. Dudziak, *Cold War Civil Rights: Race and the Image of American Democracy* (2000).
Ralph Ellison, *The Invisible Man*, (1952).
John Kenneth Galbraith, *The Affluent Society* (1958).
Sergei N. Goncahrov, John W. Lewis, and Xue Litai, *Uncertain Partners: Stalin, Mao, and the Korean War* (1993).
Juan Gonzalez, *Harvest of Empire: A History of Latinos in America* (2000).
David Halberstam, *The Fifties* (1993).
Kenneth Jackson, *Crabgrass Frontier: The Suburbanization of the United States* (1985).
Richard Kluger, *Simple Justice: The History of Brown v. Board of Education and Black America's Struggle for Equality* (1976).
Elaine Tyler May, *Homeward Bound: American Families in the Cold War Era* (1988).
Lary May, ed., *Recasting America: Culture and Politics in the Age of the Cold War* (1989).
Joanne Meyerowitz, ed., *Not June Cleaver: Women and Gender in Postwar America, 1945–1960* (1994).
James T. Patterson, *Grand Expectations: The United States, 1945–1974* (1996).
Norman Vincent Peale, *The Power of Positive Thinking* (1956).
Michael Riordan and Lillian Hoddeson, *Crystal Fire: The Birth of the Information Age* (1997).
Benjamin Spock with Dorothea Fox, *The Common Sense Book of Baby Care* (1946).
Ronald Takaki, *Strangers from a Different Shore: A History of Asian Americans* (1989).

Videos

Korea: The Forgotten War (92 minutes, Fox Hills Video, 1987). At the end of World War II, few Americans dreamed that less than five years later the nation would once again be involved in a bloody overseas conflict. Yet June 25, 1950, marked the beginning of a war like no other America had ever fought. This documentary explores that struggle, using dramatic footage captured by combat photographers and the first-person accounts of soldiers.

Korean War Stories (60 minutes, PBS Video). Although the Korean conflict is often called "The Forgotten War," it has never been forgotten by the men and women who experienced it. In this program, veterans of all types share their memories. Those interviewed include Senators John Warner and John Glenn, baseball player Ted Williams, astronaut Wally Schirra, former U.S. Secretary of State James Baker, Congressman Charles Rangel, performer Willie Nelson, NBC News correspondent Irving R. Levine, and Medal of Honor recipients General Ray Davis and Colonel Carl Sitter.

MacArthur (4 hours, PBS Video, 1999). Vain, pompous, and paranoid, General Douglas MacArthur was both admired and reviled. This documentary, originally shown as part of *The American Experience* series, shows how the liberator of the Philippines and South Korea and the supreme commander of occupied Japan could be a national hero one day and the next, a fallen soldier relieved of his powerful command.

Eisenhower/Ike (150 minutes, PBS Video, 1993). Dwight D. Eisenhower went to war an unknown soldier and returned as one of America's—and the world's— most beloved military heroes. As president during the 1950s, his talent for shrewdness as a tough "cold warrior" and skill as a wily politician belied his folksy charm. This documentary, originally produced for *The American Experience,* traces Ike's career from soldier to statesman. The program includes extensive archival footage and still photographs of World War II and the 1950s, excerpts from Eisenhower's correspondence and diaries, and interviews with biographers, historians, and family members.

Seeing Red, Stories of American Communists (100 minutes, Facets Video, 1984). Drawing on over 400 interviews with present and former American Communists, this video paints an engaging portrait of American Communism from its heyday in the 1930s through the bitter McCarthy-era witchhunts of the 1950s. It won an Academy Award nomination for Best Feature Documentary.

Point of Order (97 minutes, New Yorker Video, 1963). This powerful and at times humorous documentary excerpts coverage of the five weeks of the 1954 Army-McCarthy hearings that eventually brought down one of America's greatest political demagogues.

Cold War (20 hours, PBS Video, 1998). This twenty-four-part documentary, originally produced for CNN, uses newly released footage to tell the story of the Cold War, giving particular attention to the years from 1945 to 1960. Episodes takes the viewer inside the Pentagon, the Kremlin, and the missile sites in Cuba, to Yalta and Potsdam, Budapest and Berlin, and Hanoi and Panmunjon.

The Weapon of Choice (60 minutes, Annenberg/CPB Project, 1988). Against the backdrop of the Cold War, the Korean War, and the development of the hydrogen bomb, this documentary explores the growing reliance of the superpowers on nuclear weapons.

Divided Highways: The Interstates and the Transformation of American Life (85 minutes, Films for the Humanities and Sciences, 1997). This compelling and humorous documentary about the Interstate Highway System draws on archival material, newsreels, and interviews to describe the impact of what has been called the world's largest public works project. Dave Barry, Molly Ivins, Julia Child, Mister Rogers, Click and Clack, and many others discuss the ideals, motives, and methods of the interstate's builders, as well as the highway system's effect on community, culture, regionalism, and freedom.

David Halberstam's The Fifties (390 minutes, A&E Home Video, 1997). This six-part series, which first aired on the History Channel, portrays the 1950s as America's coming-out party—a decade-long celebration of growth and power, fueled by the Allied victory in World War II. Based on David Halberstam's best-selling book, this lively series casts a nostalgic eye back on the years of Ozzie and Harriet and the hula hoop, years which nonetheless paved the way for the tumult of the decades to follow. From Sputnik to Elvis, bobby-socks to the Kinsey Report, the documentary offers a collage of the people, music, memories, fads, and issues that sent the first baby boomers on their way.

Simple Justice (133 minutes, PBS Video, 1993). This documentary recounts the remarkable legal strategy and social struggle that resulted in the U.S. Supreme Court's landmark ruling in *Brown v. Board of Education of Topeka*. Originally produced for *The American Experience* series, it is based on Richard Kluger's prizewinning book of the same name.

Eyes on the Prize: America's Civil Rights Years, 1954–1965 (6 hours, PBS Video, 1987). This award-winning six-part series draws on extensive television footage and interviews in which movement participants recount the story of the civil rights struggle in the South. The first two episodes tell the stories of the Montgomery Bus Boycott and the struggle for school integration in the South.

Web Resources

Narratives, original documents, and web links relating to the Korean War can be found in the Truman Presidential Library's Digital Archives.
http://www.whistlestop.org/archive.htm

"The Presidents," a website hosted by PBS, offers narrative and primary sources and annotated web links related to Dwight D. Eisenhower's early career and presidency. Among the primary sources included on the site are Vice-President Richard Nixon's 1952 "Checkers" speech, documents related to the U-2 incident, the Supreme Court's decision in *Brown v. Board of Education of Topeka,* and Eisenhower's 1961 Farewell Address.
http://www.pbs.org/wgbh/amex/presidents/frames/resource/resource.html

A wealth of material on the Korean War, the Army-McCarthy hearings, and other aspects of the Cold War can be found at "Cold War," the award-winning website set up by CNN to accompany its 1998 series by the same name. The site allows visitors to navigate interactive maps, view rare archival footage online, read recently declassified documents, and tour Cold War capitals using 3-D imaging. It also offers timelines, interviews with key players, and contemporary newspaper and magazine coverage of critical events. A community bulletin board, which allows visitors to record their most vivid Cold War memories, contains scores of messages from around the globe.

http://www.cnn.com/SPECIALS/cold.war/

Webcorp presents audio clips taken from some of Senator Joseph McCarthy's red-baiting speeches. It also offers an excerpt from the stinging denunciation of McCarthy by Army Counsel Joseph Welch that helped end McCarthy's political career.

http://www.webcorp.com/mccarthy/mccarthypage.htm

"Levittown at Fifty," compiled in conjunction with a special section of New York's *Newsday,* offers visitors an intriguing look at America's most famous postwar suburb. Photographs, floor plans, newspaper advertisements, and an excerpt from a 1949 newsreel illustrate narrative histories of the development William Levitt carved out of a Long Island potato field. Highlights of the site include the recollections by some of Levittown's early residents and a copy of the Caucasians-only covenant included in lease agreements.

http://www.lihistory.com/specsec/levmain.htm

"The Literature and Culture of the American 1950s," produced by University of Pennsylvania Professor Al Filreis, is a searchable, annotated list of links to literary and cultural materials either produced during or about the 1950s. Materials range from a thirty-second ad used by the Eisenhower presidential campaign to reviews of Ralph Ellison's *Invisible Man,* from Lillian Hellman's and Allen Ginsberg's FBI files to magazine articles on American and Soviet women.

http://www.english.upenn.edu/%7Eafilreis/50s/home.html

The National Civil Rights Museum in Memphis offers a virtual interactive tour of its exhibits, using still images and panoramic views.

http://www.civilrightsmuseum.org/

CHAPTER 29 | Renewal of Reform: 1956–1968

CHAPTER OBJECTIVES

- Explain the growing concerns over U.S. national security policy in the late 1950s, as well as the differences between the Eisenhower and Kennedy administrations' approaches to foreign policy.
- Describe the "culture of dissent" that emerged among both intellectuals and adolescents in the United States during the 1950s, and discuss conservative efforts to contain such dissent.
- Trace the development and progress of the civil rights movement, the women's movement, and the environmental movement from the late 1950s through the late 1960s.
- Highlight the key stylistic and substantive issues in the presidential elections of 1960 and 1964, and account for the outcome of those elections.
- Discuss the domestic agendas and key legislative achievements of Presidents Kennedy and Johnson, and describe the differences in their political styles.
- Describe the role of the Supreme Court in the late 1950s and 1960s in promoting civil rights and civil liberties.

CHAPTER OUTLINE

I. Sputnik
   A. The Soviets' Triumph
   B. American Reactions
      1) Critique of complacency
      2) Questions about national security
II. Questions of National Security
   A. Reconsidering the Nation's Defense Strategy
      1) Emphasizing science and education

2) NASA and missile technology
3) Growing criticism of "massive retaliation"
B. Cuba
1) Castro's takeover
2) American reaction
C. U.S.-Soviet Relations
1) The "kitchen debate"
2) The U-2 incident
III. Breaking with Conformity
A. An Emerging Culture of Dissent
1) A culture of conformity
2) Critics of conformity
B. Personal Rebellion and Public License
1) Novelists and playwrights
2) Abstract expressionists
3) The Beats
4) Portrayals of sexuality
C. Young America
1) Portrayals of adolescents
2) Rock and roll
D. Censorship and the Law
1) Conservative attempts at censorship
2) Supreme Court's attack on censorship
IV. Civil Rights: Becoming a Movement
A. School Desegregation in Little Rock, Arkansas
B. Voting Rights
1) Civil Rights Act of 1957
2) Civil Rights Act of 1960
C. Sit-Ins
1) The Greensboro sit-in
2) Formation of SNCC
V. The End of the Eisenhower Era
A. Growing Discontent
B. The Election of 1960
1) Nixon vs. Kennedy
2) The campaign
C. The Eisenhower Legacy
VI. Kennedy: Idealism Without Illusions
A. Kennedy's Inauguration
B. Personal Qualities
C. Style of Governance
VII. Kennedy and the Third World
A. "Flexible Response"
B. Latin America

CHRONOLOGY

1948	Alfred Kinsey's report on male sexuality published.
1950	David Riesman publishes *The Lonely Crowd.*
1955	Bill Haley and the Comets introduce rock to national audience.
1957	Sputnik launched. Sony introduces the transistor radio. Civil Rights Act of 1957.
1957–58	School desegregation battle in Little Rock, Arkansas.
1958	National Defense Education Act. Establishment of NASA. Quiz show scandals.
1959	Castro topples Batista in Cuba. Nixon and Khrushchev engage in "kitchen debate."
1960	Greensboro sit-in and formation of SNCC. U-2 incident. DDE warns of the "military-industrial complex."
1961–63	John F. Kennedy's presidency.
1961	United States severs diplomatic relations with Cuba. Alliance for Progress announced. Bay of Pigs fiasco. CORE initiates Freedom Rides. The Berlin Crisis.
1962	Cuban Missile Crisis. Michael Harrington publishes *The Other America.* Rachel Carson publishes *Silent Spring.*
1963	Nuclear test-ban treaty. Betty Friedan publishes *The Feminine Mystique.* Assassination of Medgar Evers. Martin Luther King Jr.'s Birmingham Campaign. March on Washington. Assassination of President Kennedy.
1963–68	Lyndon B. Johnson's presidency.
1964	Passage of the Wilderness Act. Civil Rights Act of 1964. Executive order establishes affirmative action. LBJ launches the War on Poverty. "Freedom Summer" in Mississippi.
1965	Supreme Court allows use of contraceptives by married couples. Immigration Act of 1965.

	Voting Rights Act of 1965.
	Passage of Medicare and Medicaid.
1966	Formation of NOW.
1970	The first Earth Day.

ESSAY QUESTIONS

1. What factors contributed to the "culture of dissent" that emerged in the United States in the late 1950s? What role did intellectuals, artists, and youth play in this culture?

2. What was the doctrine of "flexible response"? Why did it emerge? When and how was it implemented? Be sure to give specific examples.

3. Compare the central concerns and major domestic achievements of Kennedy's New Frontier and Johnson's Great Society.

4. The civil rights movement of the 1950s and 1960s has been called America's "Second Reconstruction." Compare the Second Reconstruction to the First Reconstruction that followed the Civil War. Did it make more lasting progress? If so, why? (Consult Chapter 17 if necessary.)

5. What factors contributed to the revival of feminism in the 1960s? What goals and tactics did it share with the civil rights movement? How were the two movements different?

OBJECTIVE QUESTIONS

Multiple Choice

1. Americans reacted to the launch of Sputnik by:
   a) assuming the Soviets had the technology necessary to produce ICBMs
   b) criticizing American complacency
   c) increasing funding for science education
   d) all of the above

2. Nevil Shute's 1957 novel *On the Beach*:
   a) depicted the world after a nuclear war
   b) criticized the conformity of corporate America
   c) dramatized the world of alienated middle-class youth
   d) was banned by state and local officials for its frank portrayal of drugs and sex

3. After a brief thawing in the late 1950s, relations between the United States and the Soviet Union were plunged back into deep freeze by:

    a)   Castro's victory in the Cuban revolution

    b)   the Soviet downing of an American U-2 spy plane

    c)   an angry exchange between Vice-President Nixon and Soviet Premier Khrushchev at the American National Exhibition in Moscow

    d)   American aid to the Diem regime in South Vietnam

4. The influential book *The Lonely Crowd* was written by:
   a) Vladimir Nabokov
   b) Arthur Miller
   c) David Riesman
   d) Allen Ginsberg

5. Alfred Kinsey shocked many Americans in the 1950s by:
   a) producing bold compositions of colors and forms that bore no obvious relationship to reality
   b) celebrating sex, alcohol, and drugs in his writing
   c) reporting that half of American women had indulged in premarital sex
   d) performing what one critic called "strip-teases with clothes on"

6. The Student Non-Violent Coordinating Committee (SNCC) grew out of:
   a) the battle over school integration in Little Rock, Arkansas
   b) the sit-in movement that began in Greensboro, North Carolina, in 1960
   c) the Freedom Rides
   d) Martin Luther King Jr.'s Birmingham campaign

7. In the 1960 presidential campaign, Richard M. Nixon was hurt by all of the following except:
   a) his red-baiting past
   b) charges that a missile gap existed between the United States and the USSR
   c) Kennedy's superior use of the new medium of television
   d) the fact that he was significantly older than Kennedy

8. President Kennedy called on the United States to commit itself to "landing a man on the moon and returning him safely to earth":
   a) after the Russians beat the United States with a manned space mission
   b) in order to restore U.S. prestige among Third World nations
   c) despite the opposition of many scientists
   d) all of the above

9. All of the following were viewed as foreign policy triumphs for the Kennedy administration except:
   a) the Bay of Pigs
   b) the Berlin Crisis
   c) the Cuban Missile Crisis
   d) the nuclear test-ban treaty

10. Kennedy's chief domestic concern was:

    a)   economic growth
    b)   health care
    c)   civil rights
    d)   the environment

11. Bull Connor:
    a)   closed the public schools in Little Rock, Arkansas, rather than allowing them to desegregate
    b)   blocked James Meredith's admission to the University of Mississippi
    c)   ordered policemen to turn high-pressure water hoses on thousands of black children marching in Birmingham, Alabama
    d)   became famous for declaring "Segregation now . . . tomorrow . . . [and] forever!"

12. In the early 1960s, Newton Minnow famously used the phrase "a vast wasteland" to describe:
    a)   television
    b)   the new school of Pop Art
    c)   downtowns that had been transformed by urban renewal
    d)   wildlife refuges that had been devastated by DDT

13. The postwar environmental movement was shaped by:
    a)   spreading affluence, which allowed more people to visit national parks
    b)   Cold War imperatives that stressed the need for dynamic economic growth
    c)   growing concerns about the health risks posed by smog, pesticides, and other pollutants
    d)   all of the above

14. LBJ's legislative accomplishments included all of the following except:
    a)   the Civil Rights Act of 1964
    b)   the establishment of Medicare
    c)   the Endangered Species Act
    d)   the National Defense Education Act

15. Civil rights activists organized mass protests in Selma, Alabama in 1965 to dramatize the need for:
    a)   federal support for school desegregation
    b)   legislation outlawing racial discrimination in public accommodations
    c)   federal action on behalf of voting rights
    d)   affirmative action in hiring

True or False

1. In the late 1950s, strategic analysts increasingly criticized the doctrine of massive retaliation on the grounds that it was too expensive.

2. In the immediate aftermath of the Cuban revolution, many Americans welcomed Fidel Castro as a hero.

3. The "kitchen debate" refers to a debate between Betty Friedan and the director of the EEOC over the proper role for women in postwar America.

4. College-educated Americans who came of age in the late 1940s and early 1950s were often called the "silent generation" because they rarely spoke out on public issues and tended to avoid risk taking.

5. The Beats were a group of white musicians who helped bring the black music of rhythm and blues to a national audience.

6. The number of southern school districts embracing integration accelerated in the late 1950s and early 1960s.

7. The phrase "military-industrial complex" was coined by Dwight Eisenhower.

8. The Cuban Missile Crisis was resolved after the United States agreed to withdraw Jupiter missiles from Cuba.

9. The United States conducted far more nuclear weapons tests in the decade after it signed the nuclear test-ban treaty than it had in the previous decade.

10. In 1962, most poor Americans were white.

11. Attorney General Robert Kennedy encouraged civil rights activists to engage in direct action.

12. Andy Warhol helped create the school of Pop Art.

13. The principle of affirmative action was introduced by LBJ in a 1965 executive order.

14. The Supreme Court upheld the use of contraceptives by married couples in 1965.

15. Lyndon Johnson's Republican opponent in the 1964 presidential election was George Wallace.

SOURCES FOR FURTHER RESEARCH

Books

Irving Bernstein, *Guns or Butter: The Presidency of Lyndon Johnson* (1996).

Michael Beschloss, *The Crisis Years: Kennedy and Khrushchev, 1960–1963* (1991).

Michael R. Beschloss, ed., *Taking Charge: The Johnson White House Tapes, 1963–1964* (1997).

Taylor Branch, *Parting the Waters: America in the King Years, 1954–1963* (1988).
———, *Pillar of Fire: America in the King Years, 1963–1965* (1998).
Rachel Carson, *Silent Spring* (1962).
Robert Dallek, *Flawed Giant: Lyndon Johnson and His Times, 1961–1973* (1998).
Mary L. Dudziak, *Cold War Civil Rights: Race and the Image of American Democracy* (2000).
Sara M. Evans, *Personal Politics: The Roots of Women's Liberation in the Civil Rights Movement and the New Left* (1979).
Stephen Fox, *John Muir and His Legacy: The American Conservation Movement* (1981).
Alexksandr Fursenko and Timothy Naftali, *One Hell of a Gamble: Khrushchev, Castro, and Kennedy, 1958–1964* (1997).
Robert Gottlieb, *Forcing the Spring: The Transformation of the American Environmental Movement* (1993).
Michael Harrington, *The Other America* (1962).
Mark Harvey, *A Symbol of Wilderness: Echo Park and the American Conservation Movement* (1994).
Elizabeth Cobbs Hoffman, *All You Need Is Love: The Peace Corps and the Spirit of the 1960s* (1998).
Daniel Horowitz, *Betty Friedan and the Making of the Feminine Mystique: The American Left, the Cold War, and Modern Feminism* (1998).
Robert Hughes, *American Visions: The Epic History of Art in America* (1997).
Nicholas Lemann, *The Promised Land: The Great Black Migration and How It Changed America* (1992).
Lary May, ed., *Recasting America: Culture and Politics in the Age of the Cold War* (1989).
William McDougall, *The Heavens and the Earth: A Political History of the Space Age* (1985).
James T. Patterson, *Grand Expectations: The United States, 1945–1974* (1996).
Charles M. Payne, *I've Got the Light of Freedom: The Organizing Tradition and the Mississippi Freedom Struggle* (1995).
Rick Perlstein, *Before the Storm: Barry Goldwater and the Unmaking of the American Consensus* (2001).
Vladislav Zubok and Constantine Pleshakov, *Inside the Kremlin's Cold War: From Stalin to Khrushchev* (1996).

Videos

The Great Debates: John F. Kennedy vs. Richard M. Nixon (60 minutes, MPI Home Video, 1989). Edited selections from the four televised debates between Kennedy and Nixon during the 1960 presidential campaign. The video includes some contemporary commentary on the significance and conduct of the debates.

Cold War (20 hours, PBS Video, 1998). This twenty-four-part documentary, originally produced for CNN, uses newly released footage to tell the story of the Cold War, giving particular attention to the years from 1945 to 1960. Sputnik, the U-2 incident, the Bay of Pigs, the Berlin Wall, the Cuban Missile Crisis, and the origins of Vietnam are all discussed in various episodes.

The Bay of Pigs (57 minutes, PBS Video, 1997). Using film footage and interviews with Americans and Cubans, this video explores the Bay of Pigs incident and its long-term effect on both countries.

The JFK Tapes: Inside the Cuban Missile Crisis (22 minutes, Films for the Humanities and Sciences, 1998). This documentary, originally broadcast as part of the ABC television program *Nightline,* analyzes White House tapes recorded during the 1962 Cuban Missile Crisis. The tapes, which feature the voices of John F. Kennedy, Robert Kennedy, Dean Rusk, Curtis LeMay, Robert McNamara, and others, were released by the Kennedy Library in the 1990s.

Rachel Carson's Silent Spring (57 minutes, PBS Video, 1992). This documentary, originally broadcast as part of the PBS series *The American Experience,* offers a picture of the biologist Rachel Carson and the controversy surrounding her book *Silent Spring.*

LBJ (4 hours, PBS Video, 1991). This documentary explores the life of Lyndon Baines Johnson from his early career as a New Deal supporter to his presidency. One of America's most controversial presidents, LBJ passed a tidal wave of social legislation and scored a landslide victory in the 1964 election. However, the Vietnam War and social turmoil at home ultimately undermined Johnson's presidency, leading to his ultimate withdrawal from politics. This video includes excerpts from several of Johnson's most famous speeches.

Eyes on the Prize: America's Civil Rights Years, 1954–1965 (6 hours, PBS Video, 1987). This prizewinning six-part series draws on extensive television footage and interviews with movement participants to recount the story of the civil rights struggle in the South.

Freedom on My Mind (110 minutes, Clarity Educational Productions, 1994). Combining archival footage with contemporary interviews, this documentary of the civil rights movement focuses on the events surrounding the Mississippi Voter Registration Project of the early 1960s.

Web Resources

A wealth of material on Sputnik, the Bay of Pigs, the Berlin Wall, the Cuban Missile Crisis, and other aspects of the Cold War can be found at "Cold War," the award-winning website set up by CNN to accompany its 1998 series by the same name. The site allows visitors to navigate interactive maps, view rare archival footage online, read recently declassified documents, and tour Cold War capitals using 3-D imaging. It also offers timelines, interviews with key players, and contemporary newspaper and magazine coverage of critical events. A special interactive section on technology explores the ways in which the Cold War helped launch the space race.

http://www.cnn.com/SPECIALS/cold.war/

"The Presidents," a website hosted by PBS, offers historical narrative, primary sources, and audio clips documenting the early careers, policies, and legacies of John F. Kennedy and Lyndon B. Johnson. Original documents include letters exchanged between Kennedy, Nikita Khrushchev, and Fidel Castro during the Cuban Missile Crisis; speeches by both Kennedy and Johnson related to Vietnam and the civil rights movement; Martin Luther King Jr.'s 1963 "I Have a Dream" speech; Johnson's State of the Union addresses; and his 1965 executive order establishing affirmative action. Visitors may also listen to Kennedy's inaugural address, Johnson's key civil rights speeches to Congress, his University of Michigan address calling for the "Great Society," and his telephone conversation with George Reedy in which he revealed that he would not run for president in 1964.

http://www.pbs.org/wgbh/amex/presidents/indexjs.html

"The Literature and Culture of the American 1950s," produced by University of Pennsylvania Professor Al Filreis, is a searchable, annotated list of links to literary and cultural materials either produced during or about the 1950s. Materials range from Allen Ginsberg's FBI files to excerpts from the screenplay for *Rebel Without a Cause.*

http://www.english.upenn.edu/%7Eafilreis/50s/home.html

The "Civil Rights Documentation Project," hosted by the University of Southern Mississippi, provides a rich resource for studying the civil rights movement in that state. Visitors to the site can read transcripts of oral histories by dozens of individuals active in the movement between 1954 and 1972. The website also offers selected audio clips from these interviews, a civil rights timeline, and a bibliography of oral history interviews with civil rights activists located in archives around the country.

http://www-dept.usm.edu/~mcrohb/

The National Civil Rights Museum in Memphis offers a virtual interactive tour of its exhibits, using still images and panoramic views.

http://www.civilrightsmuseum.org/

CHAPTER 30

Years of Rage: 1964–1974

CHAPTER OBJECTIVES

- Discuss the reasons for the United States' escalating military involvement in Vietnam under Johnson, and explain the growing disillusionment with the war both among U.S. troops and Americans at home.
- Trace the emergence and decline of the antiwar movement, the New Left, and the counterculture, and compare their approaches to social and political problems.
- Explain the rising dissatisfaction of minorities of color with American society, as well as the reasons for their increasing militancy.
- Account for the resentment and disgust felt by many in "Middle America" towards those who embraced the antiwar movement, the counterculture, the sexual revolution, feminism, and various forms of minority-group militancy.
- Identify the candidates, major issues, campaign strategies, and pivotal events that shaped the elections of 1968 and 1972. Explain the outcomes of those elections.
- Describe Nixon's strategy for dealing with Vietnam, China and the Soviet Union, and the Third World, and assess the success or failure of his policies in each arena.
- Outline Nixon's approach to key domestic problems, including the economy, science funding, and the environment.
- Summarize the Nixon administration's abuses of power, including the Watergate break-in and cover-up. Understand the reasons for Nixon's eventual downfall, and the legacies of the Nixon era for American society, politics, and foreign policy.

CHAPTER OUTLINE

I.   Introduction: The Gulf of Tonkin Resolution
II.   Johnson, a Reluctant Globalist

     A. Missile Defense: ABMs and MIRVs
     B. The Middle East: The Six-Day War of 1967
     C. Latin America
        1) A rightward shift
        2) Unrest in Panama
        3) Intervention in the Dominican Republic
     D. Vietnam
        1) Johnson's conflicted views on Vietnam
        2) Stepped-up bombing and troop deployments
        3) Dubious "progress"
        4) The view from the ground
        5) Doubts and frustration

III. Upheaval at Home
     A. The Antiwar Movement
        1) Questioning the war
            a) teach-ins
            b) initial arguments against U.S. involvement
        2) The Emergence of a Movement
            a) impact of TV
            b) college campuses and the New Left
            c) attacking Defense Department funding of research
            d) calling attention to inequities in the draft
            e) novels and TV shows
     B. The Countercultural Rebellion
        1) Sources
            a) inspiration of the free-speech movement
            b) baby boom demographics
        2) Characteristics
            a) skepticism of science and reason
            b) drugs and "hippie" lifestyles
            c) role of music
        3) Losing momentum
            a) Altamont concert
            b) Manson murders
        4) Legacies to mainstream culture
            a) fashion
            b) sexual permissiveness
            c) skepticism of science and technology

IV. Militancy and Backlash
     A. Rising Fury Among Nothern Blacks
        1) Reasons
        2) Warnings of trouble to come
     B. The Fire Ignited
        1) Race riots

  2) Kerner Commission report

  3) Johnson's response

 C. Black Power

  1) The Nation of Islam and Malcolm X

  2) SNCC and the Black Panthers

  3) Culture and politics

 D. Red Power, Chicano Power

  1) Native Americans

   a) federal policy under Kennedy and Johnson

   b) "Red Power" activists

  2) Mexican Americans

   a) rural issues

   b) urban issues

 E. Backlash

  1) Defining "Middle America"

  2) Sources of resentment

V. 1968: The Politics of Protest

 A. A Turning Point

  1) The Tet offensive

  2) Political fallout

   a) rising opposition to the war

   b) Democratic challengers for the presidency

   c) Johnson's withdrawal from the race

 B. Death and Confrontation

  1) Martin Luther King Jr.'s assassination

  2) Robert F. Kennedy's assassination

  3) The 1968 Democratic convention

  4) Humphrey, Nixon, and Wallace

 C. Campaigning for Conservatism

  1) Wallace's strategy

  2) Nixon's strategy

  3) Election results and significance

VI. Nixon in the White House

 A. Nixon's Foreign Policy Strategy

 B. Henry Kissinger

VII. Exiting Vietnam

 A. The Nixon Doctrine in Theory and Practice

 B. A Prolonged War

  1) The invasion of Cambodia

  2) Renewed campus protests

  3) "Diplomacy through terror"

 C. End of the American War

  1) Terms of a cease-fire

  2) The Christmas bombings

    C. The Election of 1972
        1) Shooting of George Wallace
        2) Candidacy of George McGovern
        3) Nixon's landslide victory

XIII. Watergate
    A. The Break-In and Initial Cover-Up
        1) Break-in discovered
        2) Nixon orders a cover-up
        3) Cover-up starts to unravel
        4) The special prosecutor and the Ervin committee
        5) The battle over the tapes
        6) The "Saturday night massacre"
    B. Downfall
        1) Agnew's indictment and resignation
        2) Nixon's personal corruption
        3) Articles of impeachment
        4) The smoking gun
        5) Nixon's resignation
    C. Cold, Gray Morning: Legacies
        1) Abandoning a bipolar foreign policy framework
        2) Limiting the U.S.'s international role
        3) Abuses of power
        4) Distrust of authority
        5) Campaign finance reform

.

CHRONOLOGY

1960	Birth control pills become commercially available.
1962	SDS issues Port Huron Statement. César Chavez helps organize the National Farm Workers' Association.
1964	Gulf of Tonkin resolution. Berkeley Free Speech Movement.
1964–68	Race riots in New York, Detroit, Los Angeles, and other cities.
1965	Operation Rolling Thunder begins. University of Michigan inaugurates the teach-in. Assassination of Malcolm X.
1966	Ronald Reagan wins the California governor's race.
1967	Human Be-In in San Francisco's Golden Gate Park. 1967 Arab-Israeli War. Antiwar march on the Pentagon.

1968	Tet Offensive.
	My Lai massacre.
	Johnson withdraws from presidential race.
	Martin Luther King Jr.'s assassination.
	Robert F. Kennedy's assassination.
	Feminists demonstrate at Miss America pageant.
	Stanley Kubrick's *2001: A Space Odyssey* debuts.
	Kerner Commission reports on race riots.
	Richard M. Nixon elected president.
1969	Apollo 11 lands on the moon.
	Woodstock Festival.
	Rolling Stones's Altamont concert.
1970	Premier of M*A*S*H.
	Invasion of Cambodia.
	Kent State and Jackson State slayings.
	Establishment of the EPA.
1971	Nixon imposes wage and price controls to curb stagflation.
	New York Times publishes the *Pentagon Papers*.
	Swann v. Charlotte-Mecklenburg Board of Education.
1972	Nixon's visit to China.
	SALT Agreement signed.
	The Watergate break-in.
	Christmas bombing of North Vietnam.
1973	United States and North Vietnam negotiate settlement.
	Chile's Allende ousted in CIA-supported coup.
	Yom Kippur War.
	Ervin Committee begins Watergate hearings.
	Spiro Agnew resigns; Gerald Ford appointed vice-president.
	War Powers Act passed.
1973–74	OPEC oil embargo.
1974	House Judiciary Committee adopts articles of impeachment.
	Nixon resigns; Ford becomes president.

ESSAY QUESTIONS

1. Compare the United States' entry into the Vietnam War with its entry into World War II. What were the chief arguments made by proponents and opponents of stepped-up U.S. involvement in Vietnam? (Consult Chapters 25, 28, and 29, if necessary.)

2. The Twenties and the Sixties were both periods of intense social and cultural conflict in American society. What similarities do you see between the "cul-

ture wars" of these decades? How did they differ? Support your argument using specific examples. (Consult Chapter 23, if necessary.)

3. Why is 1968 often regarded as a pivotal year in twentieth-century American history?

4. How and why did Nixon's approach to foreign policy, in Vietnam and elsewhere, differ from that of his predecessors?

5. How did Nixon's efforts to win reelection in 1972 ultimately lead to his downfall? What were the legacies of the Watergate era for American society and politics?

OBJECTIVE QUESTIONS

Multiple Choice

1. The 1964 Gulf of Tonkin resolution:
    a) was requested by Johnson in response to a Vietcong attack on a U.S. army base at Pleiku
    b) was invoked by Johnson to legitimize stepped-up U.S. military involvement in Vietnam
    c) warned China and the USSR to stay out of the conflict in Vietnam
    d) all of the above

2. LBJ's decision to continue the war in Vietnam, despite his personal misgivings, reflected:
    a) his embrace of Eisenhower's "domino theory"
    b) his acceptance of the "lesson of Munich"—that appeasing a dictator only fosters further aggression
    c) his belief that the "loss of China" permanently eroded the effectiveness of the Truman administration
    d) all of the above

3. Agent Orange was:
    a) a chemical defoliant that the United States dropped on Vietnam to remove the enemy's ground cover
    b) an acid rock band that performed biting protest songs about the Vietnam War
    c) a psychedelic drug used by hippies to "drop out, turn on, tune in."
    d) a character in the antiwar television comedy M*A*S*H

4. "Fragging" was a slang term for:
    a) the burning of Vietnamese jungles using napalm
    b) the assassination of officers by frustrated U.S. troops in Vietnam
    c) the "free love" practices of hippies at the 1967 Human Be-In in San Francisco

d)   protest tactics engaged in by Yippies at the 1968 Democratic convention

5. In 1965, teach-ins against the Vietnam War were inaugurated at:
    a)   the University of California at Berkeley
    b)   Columbia University
    c)   the University of Michigan
    d)   Kent State University

6. The Port Huron Statement was issued by:
    a)   SDS
    b)   the Berkeley Free Speech Movement
    c)   Timothy Leary
    d)   the Black Panther Party

7. Erica Jong's *Fear of Flying*:
    a)   satirized the military
    b)   celebrated sex free of all guilt and ulterior aims
    c)   warned of the explosive resentments simmering in the black community
    d)   revealed a deep-seated skepticism of science and technology

8. The image of the counterculture as a movement devoted to love and gentleness began to change after:
    a)   the Human Be-In in San Francisco's Golden Gate Park
    b)   the Woodstock Festival in upstate New York
    c)   the Rolling Stones concert at the Altamont Speedway in California(**)
    d)   the opening of the film *Easy Rider*

9. The National Advisory Commission on Civil Disorders, headed by Illinois governor Otto Kerner, concluded that the urban riots of 1964–1968 were caused by:
    a)   juvenile delinquency
    b)   white racism
    c)   welfare programs
    d)   a handful of troublemakers

10. The Democratic Party's nomination for president in 1968 was sought by:
    a)   Eugene McCarthy
    b)   George McGovern
    c)   George Wallace
    d)   Lyndon Johnson

11. In an attempt to achieve "peace with honor" in Vietnam, Nixon:
    a)   introduced the policy of Vietnamization
    b)   opened secret peace talks in Paris with the North Vietnamese
    c)   intensified the U.S. bombing campaign against North Vietnam
    d)   all of the above

12. The wave of campus demonstrations in the spring of 1970 that ultimately resulted in the killing of six students at Kent State and Jackson State came in response to:
    a) Operation Rolling Thunder
    b) the Tet Offensive
    c) reports of the My Lai massacre
    d) the invasion of Cambodia

13. Nixon imposed wage and price controls in 1971 in an effort to tame:
    a) soaring gasoline prices
    b) stagflation
    c) a strong dollar
    d) all of the above

14. In the late 1960s, scientists compiled data showing that the most significant environmental carcinogen was:
    a) radiation from nuclear plants
    b) tobacco, when smoked
    c) the pesticide DDT
    d) asbestos

15. The "Saturday night massacre" refers to:
    a) the slaughter of civilians by U.S. troops in the Vietnamese village of My Lai
    b) the CIA-sponsored coup that lead to the death of Chilean President Salvador Allende
    c) the killing by police of two students at Jackson State University in Mississippi
    d) the firing, on Nixon's orders, of Watergate special prosecutor Archibald Cox

True or False

1. The North Vietnamese forces commanded by Ho Chi Minh were known as the Vietcong.

2. Black enlistees in the Vietnam War were twice as likely to die in action as enlisted men in general.

3. Birth control pills first became commercially available in 1960.

4. Stokeley Carmichael was an icon of the counterculture.

5. By the late 1960s, most African Americans supported violent tactics and separatism.

6. In the 1960s, only one in five Mexican Americans lived in rural areas.

7. Before the Tet Offensive, the vast majority of college students supported U.S. involvement in the Vietnam War.

8. Martin Luther King Jr. was assassinated while leading a civil rights march in Memphis, Tennessee.

9. In the 1968 presidential race, the third-party candidate won 13.5 percent of the popular vote.

10. The Nixon Doctrine ushered in the U.S. policy of détente.

11. The last manned mission to the moon occurred in 1972.

12. In the 1970s, research showed that most human cancers were caused by viruses.

13. Lyndon Johnson coined the term "silent majority" to refer to the nation's poor.

14. In *Swann v. Charlotte-Mecklenburg Board of Education,* the Supreme Court upheld the constitutionality of busing to achieve school integration.

15. Richard Nixon was ultimately forced to resign after White House tapes revealed that he had ordered the Watergate break-in of the Democratic National Committee Headquarters.

SOURCES FOR FURTHER RESEARCH

Books

David Allyn, *Make Love, Not War: The Sexual Revolution, an Unfettered History* (2000).
Stephen Ambrose, *Nixon: The Education of a Politician, 1913–1962; Nixon: The Triumph of a Politician, 1962–1972;* and *Nixon: Ruin and Recovery, 1973–1990* (1987–1991).
James Baldwin, *The Fire Next Time* (1963).
Carl Bernstein and Bob Woodward, *All the President's Men* (1974).
Irving Bernstein, *Guns or Butter: The Presidency of Lyndon Johnson* (1996).
John Morton Blum, *Years of Discord: American Politics and Society, 1961–1974* (1991).
H. W. Brands, *The Wages of Globalism: Lyndon Johnson and the Limits of American Power* (1994).
Mary C. Brennan, *Turning Right in the Sixties: The Conservative Capture of the GOP* (1995).
William F. Bundy, *The Tangled Web: The Making of Foreign Policy in the Nixon Administration* (1998).
Dan Carter, *The Politics of Rage: George Wallace, the Origins of the New Conservatism, and the Transformation of American Politics* (1995).

Matthew Dallek, *The Right Moment: Ronald Reagan's First Victory and the Decisive Turning Point in American Politics* (2000).

John D'Emilio and Estelle B. Freedman, *Intimate Matters: A History of Sexuality in America* (1988).

Fred Emery, *Watergate: The Corruption of American Politics and the Fall of Richard M. Nixon* (1994).

Todd Gitlin, *The Sixties: Years of Hope, Days of Rage* (1987).

Joan Hoff, *Nixon Reconsidered* (1994).

Maurice Isserman and Michael Kazin, *America Divided: The Civil War of the 1960s* (2000).

David Kaiser, *American Tragedy: Kennedy, Johnson, and the Origins of the Vietnam War* (2000).

Stanley Karnow, *Vietnam: A History* (1983).

Stanley Kutler, *Wars of Watergate: The Last Crisis of Richard Nixon* (1992).

Allen J. Matusow, *The Unravelling of America* (1984).

———, *Nixon's Economy: Booms, Busts, Dollars, and Votes* (1998).

Robert S. McNamara, *In Retrospect: The Tragedy and Lessons of Vietnam* (1995).

James Patterson, *Grand Expectations: The United States, 1945–74* (1996).

Kirkpatrick Sale, *The Green Revolution: The American Environmental Movement,1962–1992* (1993).

Philip Shabecoff, *A Fierce Green Fire: The American Environmental Movement* (1993).

Melvin Small, *The Presidency of Richard Nixon* (1999).

Paul Chaat Smith and Robert Allen Warrior, *Like a Hurricane: The Indian Movement from Alcatraz to Wounded Knee* (1996).

Thomas Sugrue, *The Origins of the Urban Crisis: Race and Inequality in Postwar Detroit* (1996).

Garry Wills, *Nixon Agonistes: The Crisis of the Self-Made Man* (1970).

Malcolm X, as told to Alex Haley, *The Autobiography of Malcolm X* (1990).

Videos

Making Sense of the Sixties (6 hours, PBS Video, 1991). This six-hour series examines the range of youth rebellions and shows why they developed. Part 1 recreates American society in the 1950s, focusing particularly on one of the most important seeds of rebellion: institutionalized racial prejudice. Part 2 chronicles the years 1960 to 1964, when the civil rights movement and John F. Kennedy inspired idealism in college students. Part 3 focuses on the youth rebellion and counterculture, chronicling the media's role in shaping both the rebellion and society's response. Part 4 highlights 1968, the most cataclysmic year of the decade. Part 5 examines the environmental movement, the women's movement, and splinter groups like the Black Panthers, and assesses the nation's mood at the end of the decade. Part 6 shows participants in this turbulent era reflecting on its legacies from today's perspective.

Eyes on the Prize II (8 hours, PBS Video, 1990). This eight-part sequel to the original award-winning *Eyes on the Prize* documentary carries the story of the black freedom struggle beyond 1965 as it moves out of the South. The first three hours focus on the rising sense of urgency and anger among blacks in the urban North, the influence of Malcolm X, the urban riots and Kerner Commission report, and the emergence of the Black Power movement.

Dear America: Letters Home from Vietnam (87 minutes, Ambrose Video Publishing, 1987). This moving history of America's involvement in the Vietnam War is told through the letters of American service personnel, and illustrated with contemporary news footage, home movies, and still photos.

Vietnam: A Television History (13 hours, Films for the Humanities and Sciences, 1983). This thirteen-part documentary examines America's involvement in Vietnam in the context of France's earlier colonial experience in Southeast Asia and Vietnam's 2,000-year history of resistance to foreign invaders. It draws on both archival footage and interviews with participants on all sides of the political conflict.

Nixon's China Game (60 minutes, PBS Video). This documentary tells the story of the secret White House initiative, spearheaded by Henry Kissinger, that led to a diplomatic breakthrough and ultimately President Nixon's historic 1972 trip to China. The story of this momentous event—which stunned most Americans as well as their allies and enemies—is told through the testimony of key witnesses and recently declassified records.

Nixon (3 hours, PBS Video, 1998). Originally broadcast as part of *The American Experience* series, this documentary chronicles the life and career of one of the most influential and controversial figures of the postwar era. A story of power gained, used, abused, and finally lost, this film explores the fateful combination of strengths and weaknesses that propelled Nixon to the presidency and then brought him down.

All the President's Men (155 minutes, Warner Home Video, 1998). This 1976 motion picture tells the story of how *Washington Post* reporters Carl Bernstein and Bob Woodward uncovered the White House involvement in the Watergate break-in. It is based on the book by the two men.

Web Resources

"The Wars for Viet Nam: 1945 to 1975," developed by Professor Robert Brigham of Vassar College, contains an overview of the Vietnam War, key primary sources, and links to numerous other websites with materials on Vietnam and the Vietnam

War. Brigham was the first American scholar given access to the Vietnamese archives on the war in Hanoi, and the site includes his translations of some of the documents he found.

http://vietnam.vassar.edu/

A wealth of material on the Vietnam War, the antiwar movement, détente, and the opening of China can be found at "Cold War," the award-winning website set up by CNN to accompany its 1998 series by the same name. The site allows visitors to navigate interactive maps, view rare archival footage online, read recently de-classified documents, and tour Cold War capitals using 3-D imaging. It also offers timelines, interviews with key players, and contemporary newspaper and maga-zine coverage of critical events. A community bulletin board, which allows visi-tors to record their most vivid Cold War memories, contains scores of messages from around the globe.

http://www.cnn.com/SPECIALS/cold.war/

"The Sixties Project" provides an on-line archive of scholarly articles and essays, personal narratives, primary sources, and bibliographies related to the Vietnam War, the antiwar movement, the counterculture, and other aspects of that tumul-tuous decade. The site, hosted by the Institute for Advanced Technology in the Hu-manities at the University of Virginia, also offers an extensive collection of links to related materials. Documents produced by or related to Martin Luther King Jr., the Black Panther Party, the Diggers of Haight-Ashbury, Students for a Democratic Society, the Student Non-Violent Coordinating Committee, and Vietnam Veterans Against the War are among those that can be accessed through this site.

http://lists.village.virginia.edu/sixties/HTML_docs/Sixties.html

The Smithsonian Institution's National Museum of American History offers a re-vealing look at the counterculture in "A Visual Journey: Photographs of Lisa Law, 1964–1971." The virtual exhibition, containing more than sixty of Law's pho-tographs, takes the viewer on a visual journey from the psychedelic music scene in San Francisco and Los Angeles to the family-centered and spiritual world of commune life in New Mexico. An accompanying timeline contextualizes the pho-tographs in the exhibit.

http://americanhistory.si.edu/lisalaw/1.htm

"Documents from the Women's Liberation Movement" is an on-line archival col-lection of materials held in Duke University's Special Collections Library. The materials highlight the radical origins of the women's liberation movement in the late 1960s and 1970s, and range from radical theoretical writings to humorous plays to the minutes of a grassroots feminist organization. The collection is searchable by keyword and is divided into eight subject categories: General and Theoretical, Medical and Reproductive Rights, Music, Organizations and Ac-tivism, Sexuality and Lesbian Feminism, Socialist Feminism, Women of Color, and Women's Work and Roles.

http://scriptorium.lib.duke.edu/wlm/

"Photographing History: Fred J. Maroon and the Nixon Years, 1970–1974" offers an intimate and dramatic view of the Nixon presidency and the Watergate hearings through the lens of freelance photojournalist Fred J. Maroon. In 1970, Maroon won unusual access to President Nixon with a proposal for a book on the Nixon White House. After publication of the book, he was invited to record Nixon's reelection campaign operations, and he continued to photograph the president and his milieu until Nixon's resignation in August 1974. This website, hosted by the Smithsonian Institution, also offers a detailed timeline of the Nixon years, reflections by Maroon on the art of photojournalism, and links to other relevant sites.

http://americanhistory.si.edu/maroon/index.htm

The *Washington Post*'s "Watergate 25" website includes a detailed chronology of Watergate, biographies of key players, a searchable compilation of significant articles about the scandal that appeared in the *Post,* a list of post-Watergate legislative reforms, and a discussion of the key suspects in the Deep Throat mystery. The site also offers two memoirs of life inside the newspaper at the time—one by former publisher Katherine Graham, the other by former executive editor Ben Bradlee—as well as a transcript of a live Q&A session with Bradlee and Watergate reporter Bob Woodward about the legacies of the scandal.

http://www.washingtonpost.com/wp-srv/national/longterm/watergate/front.htm

CHAPTER 31 | Conservative Revival: 1974–1980

CHAPTER OBJECTIVES

- Describe Gerald Ford's political style, and assess the successes and failures of his brief presidency.
- Summarize the symptoms of economic malaise in the United States during the 1970s, and identify the sources of that malaise.
- Discuss changing views of technology and the environment in the 1970s, including sources of both optimism and pessimism.
- Characterize Jimmy Carter's political philosophy and style, describe his key domestic concerns, and evaluate his effectiveness in dealing with them.
- Assess the Carter administration's handling of foreign affairs.
- Trace the gains made by racial and ethnic minorities, women, and gays in the 1970s, and understand the continuing challenges each group faced. Account for the anger and resistance they encountered from others in American society.
- Describe the major cultural trends of the Seventies.
- Highlight the key issues motivating conservatives in the 1970s, and account for the outcome of the 1980 presidential election.

CHAPTER OUTLINE

I. The 1970s
   A. National Pessimism
   B. A Transformative Decade
II. Ford's Stewardship
   A. Ford as President
      1) Personal traits
      2) Pardoning Nixon
   B. The Economy and Energy

    C. A Shift to Economic Conservatism
- 1) Deregulation
- 2) Increasing federal budget for R&D

    D. Energy and Inflation
- 1) The energy challenge
- 2) Carter's energy policy
- 3) Impact on oil consumption and inflation

VI. Carter and the World

    A. Reviving Idealism
- 1) Contradictions in Carter's foreign policy
- 2) Commitment to human rights
- 3) The Panama Canal

    B. The Middle East
- 1) The Camp David accords
- 2) The Iranian Revolution and hostage crisis

    C. The Soviets
- 1) Early dealings
  - a) SALT II
  - b) human rights
  - c) U.S. recognition of China
- 2) Soviet invasion of Afghanistan
  - a) background
  - b) U.S. response
- 3) Embracing a hard line
  - a) stepped-up defense spending
  - b) first-strike capability

VII. A Divided Society

    A. African Americans
- 1) Signs of progress
- 2) Growing pessimism
- 3) The urban underclass

    B. Hispanics
- 1) Official recognition as a minority group
- 2) Bilingual education
- 3) Continuing poverty

    C. Asian Americans
- 1) Post-1965 immigration
- 2) Economic divides

    D. Native Americans
- 1) Red Power and AIM
- 2) Federal policies and Supreme Court decisions

    E. Majority Resistance
- 1) Busing and desegregation
- 2) Bilingualism
- 3) Affirmative action

VIII. Fault Lines: Sexual and Cultural
- A. Women
  - 1) Feminism's expanding scope
  - 2) Backlash
- B. Gay Liberation
  - 1) Gay liberation and gay culture
  - 2) Backlash
- C. Searching for Self-Fulfillment
  - 1) Television
  - 2) Music
  - 3) Drugs
  - 4) Pop psychology
  - 5) The fitness craze
  - 6) Religion
  - 7) The "me decade"

IX. Bid for Power
- A. The Christian Right
  - 1) The Reverend Jerry Falwell
  - 2) Views of fundamentalist Protestants
  - 3) The Moral Majority
- B. A Conservative Coalition
  - 1) Economic conservatives
    - a) Tax rebellion
    - b) Sagebrush rebellion
    - c) Opposition to affirmative action
  - 2) Neoconservatives
  - 3) Social and economic conservatives: an uneasy alliance
- C. The Election of 1980
  - 1) Carter's sagging popularity
  - 2) The challengers
    - a) Edward M. Kennedy
    - b) Ronald Reagan
    - c) John Anderson
  - 3) Election results assessed

CHRONOLOGY

1969	Stonewall Riot launches gay liberation movement.
1972	Congress passes the Equal Rights Amendment.
1973	E. F. Schumacher publishes *Small Is Beautiful.*
	Siege of AIM at Wounded Knee.
	Supreme Court decision in *Roe v. Wade* legalizes abortion.

1974	Nixon resigns; Gerald Ford becomes president.
	Altair begins marketing personal computers.
1974–76	Gerald Ford's presidency.
1975	Energy Policy and Conservation Act of 1975.
	Helsinki Accords.
	Fall of Saigon.
	Mayaguez episode.
	Microsoft Corporation founded.
1976	Formation of Genentech.
	First Apple computer marketed.
1977–80	Jimmy Carter's presidency.
1977	Carter pardons draft evaders.
1978	Californians approve Proposition 13.
	Iranian revolution triggers oil price shock.
	Panama Canal Treaty.
	In *Bakke* decision, Supreme Court bans racial quotas in admissions.
1979	Iranian Revolution.
	Meltdown at Three Mile Island.
	Camp David Accords signed.
	Soviet invasion of Afghanistan.
	Reverend Jerry Falwell founds the Moral Majority.
1979–81	Iranian hostage crisis.
1980	Supreme Court approves patents on genetically modified life.
	United States boycotts Moscow Summer Olympics.
1981–88	Ronald Reagan's presidency.
1982	Vietnam Veterans Memorial completed.
	Ratification of ERA fails.

ESSAY QUESTIONS

1. What major economic problems did the United States face in the 1970s? How did Presidents Ford and Carter attempt to deal with these problems, and how successful were they?

2. Why did environmental issues become a major national concern in the 1950s, 1960s, and 1970s? How did the environmental movement evolve over the course of these decades? (Consult Chapters 29 and 30 in answering this question.)

3. What were the major foreign policy achievements and failures of the Carter administration?

4. How did Seventies culture reflect the economic and social stresses of the decade?

5. What was "new" about the New Right that emerged in the 1970s?

OBJECTIVE QUESTIONS

Multiple Choice

1. In 1974 and 1975, Henry Kissinger used "shuttle diplomacy" to forge a political settlement between:
   a) the United States and the Soviet Union
   b) Egypt and Israel
   c) North and South Vietnam
   d) the United States and Cuba

2. Saigon fell to the North Vietnamese in:
   a) 1973
   b) 1975
   c) 1977
   d) 1980

3. California's Proposition 13:
   a) slashed property taxes
   b) limited imports of certain goods
   c) banned the construction of new nuclear plants
   d) restricted research using recombinant DNA

4. All of the following contributed to the United States' economic woes in the 1970s except:
   a) high oil prices
   b) widespread labor unrest
   c) old manufacturing plants
   d) paltry expenditures on research and development

5. During the 1970s, many environmentalists:
   a) emphasized personal responsibility for the natural world
   b) saw technology as a savior
   c) allied themselves with labor and lower-income groups
   d) all of the above

6. All of the following contributed to the development of the personal computer except:
   a) military patronage of microelectronics
   b) development of the integrated circuit
   c) huge capital investments from computer companies like IBM
   d) the concentration of electronics graduates in Silicon Valley

7. Jimmy Carter:
   a) was a born-again Christian
   b) appointed many women and racial minorities to federal jobs
   c) favored voluntarism and deregulation
   d) all of the above

8. Jimmy Carter used the phrase the "moral equivalent of war" to describe:
   a) his program to combat racism and enforce civil rights
   b) his plan to reduce U.S. dependence on oil imports
   c) his human rights initiatives abroad
   d) his response to the Soviet Union's invasion of Afghanistan

9. The oil price shock of 1978–1979 which sent prices surging from 30 cents to almost $1 a gallon was triggered by:
   a) the Yom Kippur War
   b) the Iranian Revolution
   c) the accident at the Three Mile Island nuclear plant
   d) the *Mayaguez* episode

10. Jimmy Carter's foreign policy achievements included all of the following except:
    a) transferring control of the Canal Zone to Panama by 1999
    b) brokering a peace treaty between Egypt and Israel
    c) putting human rights on the world agenda
    d) passing the SALT II arms control agreement with the Soviet Union

11. Carter responded to the Soviet invasion of Afghanistan in December 1979 by:
    a) embargoing grain exports to the USSR
    b) reinstituting registration for the draft
    c) banning American participation in the 1980 Summer Olympics in Moscow
    d) all of the above

12. AIM was an acronym for:
    a) a new first-strike weapons system approved by President Carter
    b) an organization of Red Power advocates who battled federal troops at Wounded Knee, South Dakota(**)
    c) the first personal computer marketed by the Apple Corporation
    d) a self-discovery program that used encounter sessions and group touching to reveal the authentic self

13. Phyllis Schlafly:
    a) helped found the National Women's Political Caucus
    b) defeated Bobby Riggs in a much-publicized tennis match that demonstrated the athletic capabilities of women

c) sued for the right to abort her unwanted fetus, using the name "Jane Roe"

d) led the opposition to the Equal Rights Amendment

14. The mood of the Seventies was best captured in the music of:
    a) Bob Dylan
    b) Bruce Springsteen
    c) The Beatles
    d) Madonna

15. All of the following contributed to Ronald Reagan's victory in the 1980 presidential election except:
    a) the increasing politicization of fundamentalist Protestants
    b) resentment of affirmative action and federal taxation
    c) the Iranian hostage crisis
    d) high voter turnout

True or False

1. Gerald Ford was never elected to either the presidency or the vice-presidency.

2. In the 1970s, most new jobs were created in the unskilled service sector.

3. Human insulin was the first genetically engineered product to be commercially marketed.

4. Jimmy Carter's formal style alienated many on Capitol Hill.

5. In the late 1970s, the U.S. government attempted to contain the spiraling cost of energy by taxing gas-guzzling vehicles.

6. Jimmy Carter's approach to foreign policy could best be described as *realpolitik.*

7. The United States' 1980 effort to rescue the American hostages in Iran ended in disaster when the rescuers were met by hostile, rock-throwing Iranian crowds.

8. In his final two years in office, President Carter stepped up defense expenditures and initiated the largest new weapons program since before the Korean War.

9. Despite making some real economic and political gains, American blacks grew more pessimistic about their prospects in the 1970s.

10. In 1971, Mexican Americans won official recognition as a minority group with rights to special federal assistance.

11. In the 1978 *Bakke* decision, the Supreme Court ruled that a university could rely on fixed racial quotas in making its admissions decisions.

12. Even before the Supreme Court's decision in *Roe v. Wade,* some states eased anti-abortion laws.

13. Congress passed the Equal Rights Amendment in 1972, and it became the law of the land ten years later.

14. The Sagebrush Rebellion was a radical environmental group that fought for strict federal restrictions on the use of natural resources.

15. Ronald Reagan coined the term "misery index" to describe the sum of the unemployment rate and the inflation rate in the late 1970s.

SOURCES FOR FURTHER RESEARCH

Books

David Allyn, *Make Love, Not War: The Sexual Revolution, an Unfettered History* (2000).

Eric Alterman, *It Ain't No Sin to Be Glad You're Alive: The Promise of Bruce Springsteen* (1999).

Barry Bluestone and Bennett Harrison, *The Deindustrialization of America: Plant Closings, Community Abandonment, and the Dismantling of Basic Industry* (1982).

James Cannon, *Time and Chance: Gerald Ford's Appointment with History* (1994).

Jimmy Carter, *Keeping Faith: Memoirs of a President* (1982).

Martin Duberman, *Stonewall* (1993).

Alice Echols, *Daring to Be Bad: Radical Feminism in America, 1967–1975* (1989).

Gary M. Fink and Hugh Davis Graham, eds., *The Carter Presidency: Policy Choices in the Post–New Deal Era* (1998).

Ronald Formisano, *Boston Against Busing: Race, Class and Ethnicity in the 1960s and 1970s* (1991).

Paul Freiberger and Michael Swaine, *Fire in the Valley: The Making of the Personal Computer* (1984).

David Frum, *How We Got Here—The 70s: The Decade That Brought You Modern Life (For Better or Worse)* (2000).

David J. Garrow, *Liberty and Sexuality: The Right to Privacy and the Making of Roe v. Wade* (1994).

Stephen S. Hall, *Invisible Frontiers: The Race to Synthesize a Human Gene* (1987).

Jerome Himmelstein, *To the Right: The Transformation of American Conservatism* (1990).

Elsebeth Hurup, ed., *The Lost Decade: America in the Seventies* (1996).

Rebecca Klatch, *Women of the New Right* (1987).

Christopher Lasch, *The Culture of Narcissism: American Life in an Age of Diminishing Expectations* (1978).

Kristin Luker, *Abortion and the Politics of Motherhood* (1984).

Kenneth Morris, *Jimmy Carter, American Moralist* (1996).

Richard Reeves, *A Ford, Not a Lincoln* (1975).

Michael Riordan and Lillian Hoddeson, *Crystal Fire: The Birth of the Information Age* (1997).

Bruce Schulman, *The Seventies: The Great Shift in American Culture, Society, and Politics* (2001).

E. F. Schumacher, *Small Is Beautiful* (1973).

Gaddis Smith, *Morality, Reason, and Power: American Diplomacy in the Carter Years* (1986).

Winifred Wandersee, *On the Move: American Women in the 1970s* (1988).

Daniel Yergin, *The Prize: The Epic Quest for Oil, Money and Power* (1991).

Videos

We the People: The President and the Constitution: Gerald Ford (60 minutes, Anthony Potter Productions, 1991). After almost three decades in Congress, Gerald Ford was elevated to the presidency at a critical juncture. In this video, the former president discusses his pardon of Richard Nixon, the seizure of the *Mayaguez,* the summit meeting at Vladivostok, and other events of his presidency.

Carter's New World (55 minutes, PBS Video, 1989). President Carter came to office determined to improve relations between the United States and the Soviet Union and to reduce the number of nuclear weapons held by the two countries. This documentary, originally shown as part of the series *War and Peace in the Nuclear Age,* examines the events that frustrated his intentions.

We the People: The President and the Constitution: Jimmy Carter (60 minutes, Anthony Potter Productions, 1991). The first president elected from the Deep South since the Civil War, Jimmy Carter discusses the office from the perspective of a Washington outsider who sought to make human rights a centerpiece of his administration. In this interview, President Carter reflects upon the nature of presidential leadership as illustrated by the Camp David Accords, the Iran hostage crisis, the Panama Canal Treaty, the Soviet invasion of Afghanistan, and the energy crisis.

An Independent Cast of Mind (57 minutes, PBS Video, 2000). This episode of *The American President* series, focuses on four men who tried to be president without being politicians: John Adams, Zachary Taylor, Rutherford B. Hayes, and Jimmy Carter. It concludes that all had difficult presidencies.

Meltdown at Three Mile Island (60 minutes, PBS Video, 2001). This documentary, originally produced for *The American Experience,* details the events of

March 28, 1979, when a reactor at the Three Mile Island nuclear power plant in Pennsylvania overheated, sending radioactive gas and water spewing into the air. The film employs news footage and first-person interviews in telling the story of America's worst nuclear disaster.

Eyes on the Prize II: America at the Racial Crossroads, 1965–1985; Episode 7: Keys to the Kingdom (60 minutes, PBS Video, 1989). This documentary, produced by Blackside and distributed by PBS Video, traces the black freedom struggle through the difficult years of 1974 to 1980, when the legal rights gained by the civil rights movement in past decades were put to the test. In Boston, some whites violently resisted a federal school desegregation order. Atlanta's first African American mayor, Maynard Jackson, proved that affirmative action could work, but the Supreme Court's decision in the *Bakke* case challenged that policy.

Roe v. Wade (92 minutes, Paramount Pictures, 1992). This drama about the real-life Texas woman who challenged the nation's abortion law in 1973 won two Emmys.

From Danger to Dignity: The Fight for Safe Abortion (57 minutes, Concentric Media, 1995). This documentary traces the effort to legalize abortion in the United States that culminated in the Supreme Court's decision in *Roe v. Wade*. It also highlights the social and medical dangers of illegal abortions prior to that decision.

Web Resources

Visitors to the website of the Gerald R. Ford Library and Museum may view "A Day in the Life of a President," which documents April 28, 1975, the day Saigon fell to North Vietnamese forces. The site also reproduces a variety of photographs, documents, and exhibits relating to Ford's brief presidency.

http://www.ford.utexas.edu/DEFAULT.HTM

The Jimmy Carter Library and Museum offers a wide array of on-line documents and photographs, including a copy of the Camp David Accords, selected speeches given by Carter, and oral histories taken with members of the Carter family and administration. Those interested in the Iranian hostage crisis will find a report on the failed rescue mission and excerpts from a diary kept by one of the American hostages.

http://carterlibrary.galileo.peachnet.edu/

"Cold War," the award-winning website set up by CNN to accompany its 1998 series by the same name, presents historical documents and other materials relating to the Soviet invasion of Afghanistan and President Carter's response. The site also reproduces earlier correspondence between Jimmy Carter and Soviet leader Leonid Brezhnev as they sought to reduce Cold War tensions.

http://www.cnn.com/SPECIALS/cold.war/

"Camp David Accords: Framework for Peace," a virtual exhibit produced by the Presidential Libraries IDEA Network and the Jimmy Carter Library, explores the 1978 Camp David negotiations between Egypt and Israel, as well as their inception and legacy.

> http://www.ibiblio.org/sullivan/CampDavid-Accords-homepage.html

"Documents from the Women's Liberation Movement" is an on-line archival collection of materials held in Duke University's Special Collections Library. The materials highlight the radical origins of the women's liberation movement in the late 1960s and 1970s, and range from radical theoretical writings to humorous plays to the minutes of a grassroots feminist organization. The collection is searchable by keyword and is divided into eight subject categories: General and Theoretical, Medical and Reproductive Rights, Music, Organizations and Activism, Sexuality and Lesbian Feminism, Socialist Feminism, Women of Color, and Women's Work and Roles.

> http://scriptorium.lib.duke.edu/wlm/

CHAPTER 32

The Reagan Revolution: 1980–1988

CHAPTER OBJECTIVES

- Characterize Ronald Reagan's political philosophy and presidential style.
- Explain Reagan's approach to managing the economy, including "supply-side economics," the New Federalism, and deregulation. Assess the impact of his approach on various socioeconomic groups, on different industries and localities, and on the economy as a whole.
- Highlight the key elements of Reagan's foreign policy vis-à-vis the Soviet Union and the Third World. Discuss how and why his approach to the Soviet Union evolved over time.
- Understand the ingredients of the Iran-Contra scandal, and its relationship to Reagan's foreign policy goals.
- Describe the impact of the Reagan era on unions, the women's movement, people of color, and the space program.
- Summarize the health and environmental problems facing Americans during the 1980s, and discuss the Reagan administration's approach to addressing those problems.
- Highlight the key stylistic and substantive issues in the presidential elections of 1984 and 1988, and account for the outcome of those elections.

CHAPTER OUTLINE

I.   Ronald Reagan
    A.   Biography
    B.   Personality
    C.   Nancy Reagan
    D.   Political Style
II. Reaganomics
    A.   Supply-Side Economics

       1) The theory
       2) Recession and recovery
       3) Slashing spending on social programs
       4) New Federalism
       5) Cuts in funding for education
   B. Deficits
       1) Reasons for huge deficits
       2) Positions of political parties
       3) Borrowing from abroad
   C. Deregulation
       1) Deregulation accelerates under Reagan
       2) Impact
          a) S&Ls
          b) airlines
          c) telephone industry
          d) health and safety
          e) the environment
       3) Opposition from social conservatives
III. Reagan, the Soviets, and Nuclear Weapons
   A. The Soviets and the U.S. Strategic Arsenal
       1) The "evil empire"
       2) Reagan's belief in a missile gap
       3) Mushrooming defense outlays
   B. Star Wars
       1) The nuclear freeze movement
       2) SDI
       3) Federal spending on R&D
   C. Affirmation: The Election of 1984
       1) The candidates
       2) Reagan's landslide victory
IV. Reagan and the Third World
   A. The Reagan Doctrine
   B. Stalemate and Terror: The Middle East
       1) Israel, the Palestinians, and Lebanon
       2) Libya
   C. Central America
       1) Nicaragua
       2) Grenada
   D. Scandal: Iran-Contra
       1) Arms-for-hostages in Iran
       2) Illegal aid to the Contras
       3) Cover-up
       4) Congressional hearings and indictments
       5) Negotiated settlement in Nicaragua

    E. Flexibility: Africa, the Philippines, and Haiti
- 1) South Africa
- 2) The Philippines
- 3) Haiti

V. Doing Business with the Soviets
    A. A Fresh Start
- 1) Mikhail Gorbachev
- 2) The Geneva summit

    B. Setback over Star Wars

    C. The Making of a Miracle
- 1) Gorbachev's shift on SDI
- 2) Gorbachev's internal reforms
- 3) The INF Treaty
- 4) "Gorbymania"

VI. Reagan's America
    A. Greed Is Good
- 1) Signs of prosperity
- 2) "Yuppies," celebrities, and junk bond dealers
- 3) Televangelists
- 4) Tax cuts for the wealthy

    B. Stresses in the Workforce
- 1) Air traffic controllers' strike
- 2) Declining union membership
- 3) Mergers, takeovers, and corporate restructurings
- 4) Decline of smokestack industries
- 5) Farm Belt woes
- 6) Foreign trade
- 7) Falling wages
- 8) The working poor

    C. Women
- 1) Wage and salary increases
- 2) Status gains
- 3) Backlash against feminism
  - a) men's resentment
  - b) social conservatives
  - c) younger women
- 4) Evolving feminist agenda
  - a) Betty Friedan's *Second Stage*
  - b) parental leave

    D. Peoples of Color
- 1) Widening socioeconomic divisions
- 2) Native minorities
  - a) advances
  - b) impact of Reagan's policies

      3) Immigrant minorities
         a) scope of legal and illegal immigration
         b) economics and politics
         c) culture
         d) comparison to earlier waves
         e) reception

VII. Troubles in the Good Life
   A. Variations on the Good Life
      1) Migration
         a) to the Sunbelt
         b) to the suburbs
      2) Technology
      3) Escaping urban problems
   B. The *Challenger* Disaster
      1) The space shuttle program
      2) The *Challenger* explosion
   C. Medicine and Public Health
      1) Advances in medical imaging: CT-scans and MRIs
      2) Increased funding for biomedical research
      3) Rising costs of medical care
      4) Public health hazards
         a) smoking and drugs
         b) AIDS
      5) The environment, local and global
         a) grass-roots activism
         b) new danger: ozone depletion

VIII. Political Reckoning
   A. Undercurrent of Disquiet
      1) 1986 elections
      2) Supreme Court appointments
   B. The Election of 1988
   C. The Reagan Legacy

CHRONOLOGY

1981–88	Ronald Reagan's presidency.
1981	Reagan survives assassination attempt.
	Reagan's initial tax cut implemented.
	Sandra Day O'Connor appointed to the Supreme Court.
	CIA begins aiding Nicaraguan Contras.
	Reagan fires striking air traffic controllers.
	Betty Friedan publishes *Second Stage*.

1982	Unemployment peaks at nearly 10 percent.
	Federal judge orders breakup of AT&T.
	Nuclear freeze movement stages rally in Central Park.
1983	Secretary of the Interior James Watt resigns.
	Reagan announces Strategic Defense Initiative.
	Suicide truck bomber in Beirut kills 241 marines.
	United States invades Grenada.
1984	U.S. and French researchers identify HIV as cause of AIDS.
1985	United States becomes a debtor nation for first time since 1914.
	Reagan and Gorbachev meet at Geneva summit.
1986	Iran-Contra scandal breaks.
	Condemning apartheid, Congress bans all imports from South Africa.
	Philippine president Ferdinand Marcos flees to the United States.
	Reykjavik Summit ends in disappointment.
	Gorbachev introduces *glasnost* and *perestroika*.
	Reagan's Tax Reform Act passed.
	Supreme Court rules against sexual harassment in the workplace.
	Congress passes Immigration Reform and Control Act.
	Space shuttle *Challenger* explodes after lift-off.
1987	Stock market crash.
	Palestinians launch the first *intifada*.
	Reagan and Gorbachev sign INF Treaty.
1988	Bomb downs Pan Am jet over Lockerbie, Scotland.
1989–92	George Bush's presidency.
1989	Supreme Court allows broader state regulation of abortion.

ESSAY QUESTIONS

1. How did Ronald Reagan's political style differ from that of his predecessor, Jimmy Carter? Do you see any similarities between the two presidents?

2. What did conservative theorists mean by "supply-side economics," and how did Reagan implement their theories? Who benefited from "Reaganomics," and who was hurt by it? How effective was it at solving the nation's overall economic woes?

3. What was the Iran-Contra scandal, and how did it reflect President Reagan's overall approach to foreign policy?

4. How and why did relations between the United States and the Soviet Union change during the Reagan years?

5. Some observers have compared the 1980s to the 1920s. What similarities and differences do you see between these decades? (Consult Chapter 23 if necessary.)

OBJECTIVE QUESTIONS

Multiple Choice

1. "Just Say No" was the slogan of the Reagan administration's:
   a) campaign against premarital sex
   b) campaign against drugs
   c) campaign against big government
   d) campaign against higher taxes

2. Reagan's economic policies:
   a) sought to stimulate the economy by cutting taxes
   b) resulted in ballooning federal deficits
   c) were described by Reagan's vice-president as "voodoo economics"
   d) all of the above

3. Reagan used the phrase "the evil empire" to describe:
   a) the Soviet Union
   b) Iran
   c) Nicaragua
   d) Libya

4. The 1984 Democratic vice-presidential nominee was:
   a) Lloyd Bentsen
   b) Walter Mondale
   c) Geraldine Ferraro
   d) Jeane Kirkpatrick

5. The Reagan Doctrine held that the United States should:
   a) support anti-Communist "freedom fighters" in the Third World
   b) close the "window of vulnerability" with the Soviet Union
   c) support peace efforts in the Middle East
   d) avoid committing U.S. ground troops overseas

6. The Iran-Contra scandal encompassed:
   a) selling antitank missiles to Iran in exchange for American hostages
   b) providing illegal aid to Nicaraguan rebels
   c) a cover-up by key members of the Reagan administration
   d) all of the above

7. Corazon Aquino led the democratic opposition in:
   a) El Salvador
   b) the Philippines
   c) Nicaragua
   d) Grenada

8. The 1987 INF Treaty between the United States and the Soviet Union was:
   a) initially proposed by Mikhail Gorbachev
   b) the first to abolish an entire class of nuclear weapons
   c) signed at a time specified by Nancy Reagan's astrologer
   d) all of the above

9. When two-thirds of the nation's air traffic controllers went on strike in 1981, Reagan:
   a) agreed to pay them higher wages
   b) agreed to submit their demands to arbitration
   c) imposed a two-month "cooling off" period
   d) fired them

10. The prosperity of the Reagan years contributed to:
    a) a decline in homelessness
    b) a rise in the real hourly wages paid workers
    c) an increased concentration of wealth in the hands of the wealthy
    d) all of the above

11. The term "model minority" was coined to refer to:
    a) Jewish Americans
    b) African Americans
    c) Native Americans
    d) Asian Americans

12. Budgetary cutbacks during the Reagan era slashed funding for all of the following except:
    a) the school lunch program
    b) Indian health and education
    c) NASA's space shuttle program
    d) biomedical research

13. The Montreal Protocol signed in 1987:
    a) was designed to stem the flow of illegal immigrants
    b) imposed international controls on chemicals that deplete the ozone layer
    c) called for "constructive engagement" with South Africa
    d) gave Canada "Most Favored Nation" trading status

14. Reagan successfully nominated all of the following to the Supreme Court except

a) Sandra Day O'Connor
b) Antonin Scalia
c) Robert Bork
d) Anthony Kennedy

15. The presidential candidate who called for a "kinder, gentler America" was:
a) Ronald Reagan in 1980
b) Walter Mondale in 1984
c) George Bush in 1988
d) Michael Dukakis in 1988

True or False

1. The national debt nearly tripled during Ronald Reagan's years in office.

2. Reagan's policies of deregulation contributed to the failure of numerous Savings and Loans.

3. Ronald Reagan's domestic agenda dovetailed with that of social conservatives like Jerry Falwell.

4. In 1981, Reagan directed the CIA to begin arming the Sandinistas.

5. Reagan sent U.S. marines into Haiti in 1983.

6. Gorbachev restructured the Soviet economy to encourage private entrepreneurship, in a move known as *perestroika.*

7. "Junk bonds" allowed corporate raiders to purchase corporations for prices far higher than the corporations were worth.

8. The tax cuts instituted by the Reagan administration primarily benefited middle- and working-class Americans.

9. In the 1980s, the median salaries of women rose, while those of men fell.

10. The Immigration Reform and Control Act of 1986 extended amnesty to thousands of illegal aliens.

11. By the late 1980s, Hispanics were more likely to have completed high school than were African Americans.

12. In 1990, almost half of all Americans lived in suburbia.

13. Christa McAuliffe was the first female astronaut.

14. Women were more heavily represented in the grass-roots environmental movement than were men.

15. Reagan's Strategic Defense Initiative, known as "Star Wars," forced the Soviet Union to agree to a reduction in strategic nuclear weapons.

SOURCES FOR FURTHER RESEARCH

Books

Michael Beschloss and Strobe Talbott, *At the Highest Levels: The Inside Story of the End of the Cold War* (1993).

Sidney Blumenthal and Thomas B. Edsall, eds., *The Reagan Legacy* (1988).

Lou Cannon, *President Reagan: The Role of a Lifetime* (1991).

Theodore Draper, *A Very Thin Line: The Iran-Contra Affairs* (1991).

Robert Dallek, *Ronald Reagan: The Politics of Symbolism* (1984).

Mike Davis, *City of Quartz: Excavating the Future in Los Angeles* (1992).

Thomas Byrne Edsall with Mary D. Edsall, *Chain Reaction: The Impact of Race, Riots and Taxes on American Politics* (1991).

Barbara Ehrenreich, *The Worst Years of Our Lives: Irreverent Notes from a Decade of Greed* (1990).

Susan Faludi, *Backlash: The Undeclared War Against American Women* (1991).

Frances Fitzgerald, *Way Out There in the Blue: Reagan, Star Wars and the End of the Cold War* (2000).

John Lewis Gaddis, *The United States and the End of the Cold War: Implications, Reconsiderations, Provocations* (1992).

———, *We Now Know: Rethinking Cold War History* (1997).

Joel Garreau, *Edge City: Life on the New Frontier* (1991).

Benett Harrison and Barry Bluestone, *The Great U-Turn: Corporate Restructuring and the Polarizing of America* (1988).

James D. Hunter, *Culture Wars: The Struggle to Define America* (1991).

Haynes Johnson, *Sleepwalking Through History: America in the Reagan Years* (1991).

Alex Kotlowitz, *There Are No Children Here: The Story of Two Boys Growing Up in the Other America* (1991).

Michael Lewis, *Liar's Poker: Rising Through the Wreckage on Wall Street* (1989).

Michael Lienesch, *Redeeming America: Piety and Politics in the New Christian Right* (1993).

Martin Lowy, *High Rollers: Inside the Savings and Loan Debacle* (1991).

Peggy Noonan, *What I Saw at the Revolution: A Political Life in the Reagan Era* (1990).

Keven Phillips, *The Politics of Rich and Poor: Wealth and the American Electorate in the Reagan Aftermath* (1990).

Michael Schaller, *Reckoning with Reagan: America and Its President in the 1980s* (1991).

Randy Schilts, *And the Band Played On: Politics, People, and the AIDS Epidemic* (1987).

James B. Stewart, *Den of Thieves* (1991).

David Stockman, *The Triumph of Politics: How the Reagan Revolution Failed* (1986).

Diane Vaughan, *The Challenger Launch Decision: Risky Technology, Culture, and Deviance at NASA* (1996).
Garry Wills, *Reagan's America: Innocents at Home* (1987).
William Julius Wilson, *The Truly Disadvantaged: The Inner City, the Underclass, and Public Policy* (1987).
Bob Woodward, *Veil: The Secret Wars of the CIA, 1981–1987* (1987).

Videos

Conservatives (88 minutes, Films for the Humanities and Sciences, 1993). This program traces the rise of the conservative movement in America from the 1940s through the Reagan era. Among other things, it discusses Reagan's ideological evolution, the birth of neo-conservatism, the impact of Watergate, the emergence of the New Right, and the influence of supply-side economics.

Reagan (5 hours, PBS Video, 1998). This documentary tells Ronald Reagan's life story, with comments from contemporaries and historians.

Ronald Reagan: The Great Communicator (340 minutes, MPI Home Video, 1999). This four-part series offers an overview of the Reagan presidency using clips of presidential appearances, as well as rare newsreel and archival footage from the Reagan Library. The documentary examines Reagan's life before he entered the White House; discusses the "Reagan Revolution," including his fight against government waste and high taxes; and analyzes America's relationship with the Soviet Union during his presidency.

Reagan's Shield and *Zero Hour* (55 minutes each, PBS Video, 1989). These documentaries were originally produced for the PBS series *War and Peace in the Nuclear Age*. The first focuses on Reagan's controversial Strategic Defense Initiative, an idea Reagan believed would make nuclear weapons "impotent and obsolete." The second discusses the steps that led Reagan and Gorbachev to sign the INF agreement, eliminating an entire class of nuclear weapons from Europe.

Cold War (20 hours, PBS Video, 1998). This twenty-four-part documentary, originally produced for CNN, uses newly released footage to tell the story of the Cold War. Episode 18, "Backyard: 1950–1990," discusses U.S. efforts to destabilize leftist governments in Latin America, including El Salvador, Nicaragua, and Grenada. Episode 22, "Star Wars: 1980–1988," discusses Reagan's plan to place an anti-missile system in space, as well as the Soviet response.

High Crimes and Misdemeanors (90 minutes, PBS Video, 1990). This documentary, originally produced for the *Frontline* series, summarizes the covert operations that became the Iran-Contra Affair. It examines the Reagan administration's involvement in the arms-for-hostages swap, and explains the role played by Iran, Israel, and Nicaragua.

Wall Street (126 minutes, FoxVideo, 1992). This 1986 motion picture captures the culture of avarice that pervaded much of the financial sector during the Reagan years, as well as the fradulent activites that eventually came to light. Bud Fox is an ambitious young Wall Street broker whose quest for new clients leads him to Gordon Gekko, a financial wizard with a genius for making money. Gekko lures Fox into the illegal but lucrative world of corporate espionage and insider trading.

Eyes on the Prize II (8 hours, PBS Video, 1990). This eight-part sequel to the original award-winning *Eyes on the Prize* documentary carries the story of the black freedom struggle beyond 1965 as it moves out of the South. Episode 8 deals with the years from 1979 to the mid-1980s. Miami's black community, which had suffered through urban renewal, a lack of jobs and police harrassment, ultimately exploded in rioting. In Chicago, meanwhile, an unprecedented grass-roots movement triumphed. Frustrated by decades of unfulfilled promises made by the city's Democratic political machine, reformers installed Harold Washington as the city's first black mayor.

Thinking Machines: The Creation of the Computer (50 minutes, A&E Home Video, 1995). This documentary traces the evolution of the computer from the 1970s through the 1990s.

And the Band Played On (140 minutes, HBO Pictures, 1993). This drama about the early months of the AIDS epidemic is based on Randy Shilts's best-selling book by the same name. In the summer of 1981, little was known about the disease we now call AIDS. This movie follows the struggle of a handful of strong-willed men and women who took on the fight to save lives.

Web Resources

The Ronald Reagan Presidential Library reproduces scores of Reagan's speeches and other public papers in a format that can either be browsed by date or searched by keyword. The library also offers biographical information on both Ronald and Nancy Reagan, as well as dozens of formal and informal photographs on subjects ranging from Reagan's summits with Gorbachev to the Iran-Contra scandal to the attempt to assassinate the president.

http://www.reagan.utexas.edu/resource.htm

"The Presidents," a website hosted by PBS, offers historical narrative, primary sources, and audio clips documenting the early career, policies, and legacy of Ronald Reagan. Original documents include Reagan's inaugural and farewell addresses, the 1982 speech in which he dubbed the Soviet Union "the evil empire," his 1986 address to the nation following the *Challenger* disaster, and his 1987 speech addressing the Iran-Contra scandal. Visitors may also listen to interviews on a variety of subjects with Nancy Reagan, Mikhail Gorbachev, and Reagan's chief of staff James Baker. The site also contains a synopsis of the era, a bibliograhy, and links to related sites.

http://www.pbs.org/wgbh/amex/presidents/indexjs.html

The Internet Public Library's "Presidents of the United States Site (POTUS)" offers extensive material on each of the nation's forty-three presidents. The portion of the site dedicated to Ronald Reagan contains election results of the 1976, 1980 and 1984 presidential elections, a list of Reagan's cabinet members, a personal fact sheet on the president, links to other political figures and presidents, material on First Lady Nancy Reagan, a sound and image file, primary sources, and links to other related sites.

http://www.ipl.org/ref/POTUS/rwreagan.html

"Cold War," the companion website to CNN's 1998 series of the same name, offers a collection of materials on the U.S. invasion of Grenada, U.S. involvement with Nicaragua and El Salvador, Reagan's Strategic Defense Initiative (SDI), and the Soviet response to SDI. Visitors can read the CIA's 1983 "Freedom Fighter" manual for Nicaraguan Contra rebels, view e-mail exchanged between John Poindexter and Oliver North as they plotted ways to funnel secret aid to the Contras, and listen to interviews with leaders of both the Contras and the Sandinistas. The site also contains the text of Reagan's "Star Wars" speech, audio clips from an interview with Gorbachev about SDI, and contemporary coverage in both *Time* and *Pravda*.

http://www.cnn.com/SPECIALS/cold.war/

On January 28, 1986, the space shuttle *Challenger* exploded during lift-off, killing all seven crew members. "The Challenger Accident" homepage, created by the Space Policy Project of the Federation of American Scientists, offers links to a variety of Internet sites with material on the disaster. Materials include original video clips of the accident, Reagan's subsequent speech to the nation, and excerpts from the report of the presidential commission appointed to investigate the tragedy.

http://www.fas.org/spp/51L.html

CHAPTER 33

Triumphant and Troubled Nation: 1989–2000

CHAPTER OBJECTIVES

- Trace the string of events between 1989 and 1991 that marked the end of the Cold War, and discuss the factors that contributed to its end.
- Describe the foreign policy challenges that the United States faced in the wake of the Cold War, and explain how George Bush and Bill Clinton dealt with those challenges.
- Summarize the causes and consequences of the Gulf War.
- Discuss the domestic policies of the Bush and Clinton administrations, and compare the achievements and failures of the two presidents.
- Highlight the central issues in the elections of 1992, 1994, and 1996, and account for the outcome of those elections.
- Characterize the economic boom of the 1990s.
- Understand the sources and manifestations of conservative resentment in the 1990s.
- Summarize the circumstances that led to Bill Clinton's impeachment, and assess the impact of that episode on his legacy.

CHAPTER OUTLINE

I.   Post–Cold War Challenges
II. Foreign Affairs
    A.   George Herbert Walker Bush: Biography
    B.   The End of the Cold War
        1)   Central and Eastern Europe
        2)   The demise of the Soviet Union
    C.   Ripples of Freedom
        1)   South Africa

      2) The Third World
        a) Nicaragua
        b) El Salvador
        c) Panama
      3) China
   D. The Gulf War
      1) The Iraqi invasion of Kuwait
      2) U.S. response
        a) mobilizing a coalition
        b) sending troops to Saudi Arabia
        c) the U.N. resolution
        d) the war against Iraq
        e) terms of the armistice
      3) Middle East peace: some reasons for hope
III. A Domestic Guardian
   A. Bush's Lack of Vision
      1) A "guardianship" presidency
      2) Emphasis on voluntarism
   B. The Troubled Economy
      1) S&L crisis
      2) Federal deficit
      3) Recession
        a) causes
        b) Bush's proposed solutions
   C. Civil Rights
      1) Appointments of minorities and women
      2) Americans with Disabilities Act
      3) Los Angeles riot
      4) Affirmative action
   D. The Supreme Court
      1) Appointment of David Souter
      2) Thomas-Hill controversy
      3) Court's growing conservatism
   E. Health and the Environment
      1) A War on Drugs
      2) The environment: pollution and warming
   F. The Election of 1992
      1) Bill Clinton: style and issues
      2) George Bush: issues and troubles
      3) H. Ross Perot
      4) Outcome
IV. The Clinton Presidency
   A. Bill Clinton
      1) Biography

        2) Political style
        3) Agenda
    B. The Economy and Free Trade
        1) Clinton's tax-and-spending package
        2) Battle over NAFTA
        3) A reviving economy
        4) The World Trade Organization
    C. Setbacks: Health Care and Gay Rights
        1) Battle over universal health care
        2) Homosexuals and women in the military
    D. Elections, 1994: A Republican Earthquake
        1) Anti-crime and welfare reform bills
        2) The 1994 midterm elections
            a) questions about Clinton's character
            b) Newt Gingrich and the "Contract with America"
            c) Republican landslide
        3) The 104th Congress
        4) Clinton's response
            a) federal government shutdowns
            b) emphasizing budget balancing and debt reduction
            c) welfare reform
    E. The 1996 Election
        1) Bob Dole and the Republican campaign
        2) Evidence of economic abundance
        3) Clinton's victory
V. The Post–Cold War World
    A. Clinton's Foreign Policy: "Democratic Enlargement"
    B. Russia
        1) Financial assistance
        2) Nuclear stockpiles and missiles
    C. Violence in the Former Yugoslavia
        1) Serbia, Croatia, and Bosnia
        2) Kosovo
    D. China and the Pacific Rim
        1) Trade issues
        2) Recognizing Vietnam
        3) China
        4) North Korea
    E. Peacemaking in Haiti and Northern Ireland
        1) Haiti
        2) Northern Ireland
    F. Failure in Somalia and Rwanda
        1) Somalia
        2) Rwanda
    G. The Middle East and the Spread of Terror

      2) Crime and the schools
         a) declining crime rate
         b) school shootings
  H. Resentments
      1) Sources of conservative resentment
         a) religious and family issues
         b) affirmative action
      2) Violent confrontations
         a) siege at Ruby Ridge
         b) battle at Waco
         c) the Oklahoma City bombing
VII. Renewing the Domestic Agenda
  A. A Cautious Approach
      1) Campaign finance reform
      2) Budget surplus
  B. Gun Control, the Environment, and Tobacco
      1) Failure of gun control legislation
      2) Environmental issues
      3) Tobacco industry settlement
  C. Sex, Lies, and Impeachment
      1) The Lewinsky scandal
         a) the Starr investigation
         b) Paula Jones and Monica Lewinsky
      2) Tightening the noose
         a) Clinton's denials
         b) Lewinsky's testimony
         c) impeachment inquiry
      3) Slipping through
         a) public opinion
         b) House impeachment
         c) Senate acquittal
      4) The Clinton record

CHRONOLOGY

1989–92	George Herbert Walker Bush's presidency.
1989–90	Collapse of Communist regimes in Central and Eastern Europe.
1989	Oil tanker *Exxon Valdez* runs aground in Alaska.
	Chinese massacre dissidents in Tiananmen Square.
	U.S. troops invade Panama and oust Manual Noriega.

1990	Bush signs the Americans with Disabilities Act.
	Iraq invades Kuwait.
	David Souter named to the Supreme Court.
1991	Persian Gulf War.
	Clarence Thomas/Anita Hill controversy.
	Soviet Union dissolves.
1992	White South Africans vote to end apartheid.
	U.S. recession begins.
	Siege of white separatist at Ruby Ridge, Idaho.
	Rodney King case leads to Los Angeles riot.
1993–2000	William Jefferson Clinton's presidency.
1993	Muslim terrorists explode car bomb in World Trade Center garage.
	Federal agents battle Branch Davidians in Waco, Texas.
	Military institutes "Don't ask, don't tell" policy on gays.
	Israel and PLO sign the Oslo Accords.
	U.S. Army Rangers ambushed in Somalia.
	Congress approves NAFTA Treaty.
	Toni Morrison wins Nobel Prize in Literature.
1994	Kenneth Starr appointed special prosecutor to look into Whitewater.
	Republicans win landslide in midterm elections.
	World Trade Organization (WTO) created.
	Croatian, Serbian, and Bosnian leaders sign Dayton peace accords.
	Netscape launched.
1995	United States normalizes relations with Vietnam.
	Timothy McVeigh bombs the Oklahoma City federal building.
	Louis Farrakhan leads the "Million Man March" in Washington, D.C.
1996	Welfare reform act passed.
	Californians pass initiative ending racial preferences in college admissions.
1998	Lewinsky sex scandal breaks; Clinton denies allegations.
	Suicide truck bombers blow up U.S. embassies in Tanzania and Kenya.
	Clinton brokers Wye Memorandum between Israel and Palestinians.
	States reach $206 billion settlement with tobacco industry.
	House impeaches Clinton for perjury and obstruction of justice.

1999	Senate acquits Clinton on all charges.
	School schooting at Columbine High School leaves thirteen dead.
	United States achieves balanced federal budget.
2000	Terrorists linked to bin Laden attack the USS *Cole* in Yemen.
	Mapping of the human genome completed.

ESSAY QUESTIONS

1. For more than four decades, the Cold War cast a broad shadow across American life. How did the end of the Cold War affect both the U.S. economy and American foreign policy? How did Presidents Bush and Clinton respond to the new challenges?

2. When Bill Clinton ran for president in 1992 he presented himself as a "New Democrat." What did he mean by that? How did his domestic agenda and policies differ from those of his Democratic predecessors? (Consult earlier chapters if necessary.)

3. What accounted for the economic boom of the 1990s? Who benefited most and who was left behind?

4. Why was President Clinton impeached in 1999? In answering this question, consider both specific events and broader cultural trends. How do you think Clinton's impeachment will affect his legacy?

5. In what sense could the United States at the end of the 1990s be considered "two nations"? Were the deepest divisions racial, economic, or cultural? To what degree did these divisions overlap?

OBJECTIVE QUESTIONS

Multiple Choice

1. All of the following occurred in 1989 except:
   a) Communist regimes across Central Europe collapsed
   b) the Berlin Wall was torn down
   c) the Soviet Union dissolved
   d) Chinese troops massacred dissidents in Tiananmen Square

2. In 1989, President Bush sent U.S. troops into:
   a) Angola
   b) Namibia
   c) Nicaragua
   d) Panama

3. The Gulf War began after:
   a) Iraq invaded Kuwait
   b) Iraq invaded Saudi Arabia
   c) Iraq launched Scud missiles at Israeli cities
   d) Iraq refused to sell oil to the United States

4. All of the following phrases are associated with President Clinton except:
   a) "a thousand points of light"
   b) "It's the economy, stupid"
   c) "The Comeback Kid"
   d) "I feel your pain"

5. In an effort to deal with the nation's mounting economic problems, President Bush:
   a) strengthened federal oversight of savings and loan institutions
   b) raised taxes
   c) negotiated the North American Free Trade Agreement
   d) all of the above

6. Controversy erupted when George Bush nominated to the Supreme Court:
   a) David Souter
   b) Clarence Thomas
   c) Rodney King
   d) William Bennett

7. President Bush responded to the threat of global warming by:
   a) imposing major restrictions on the burning of fossil fuels
   b) offering incentives for research and development on solar power
   c) encouraging construction of nuclear power plants
   d) questioning the link between carbon dioxide emissions and global warning

8. The pivotal issue in the 1992 presidential election was:
   a) Clinton's sexual dalliances
   b) the state of the economy
   c) reproductive choice
   d) U.S. policy towards "the former Soviet Union"

9. During his first term, Clinton scored legislative victories in all of the following arenas except:
   a) promoting free trade
   b) providing universal health care
   c) reforming the welfare system
   d) combatting crime

10. The Republicans were hurt in the 1996 elections by:
    a) the partial shutdown of the federal government

   b)   the "Contract for America"
   c)   their nomination of H. Ross Perot for president
   d)   all of the above

11. During the 1990s, the United States sent peacekeeping troops into all of the following except:
   a)   Bosnia
   b)   Kosovo
   c)   Haiti
   d)   Rwanda

12. During the 1990s, many Middle Eastern Muslims were angered by:
   a)   U.S. support for continuing economic sanctions against Iraq
   b)   the presence of American troops in Saudi Arabia after the Gulf War
   c)   U.S. support for Israel
   d)   all of the above

13. The 1995 "Million Man March" in Washington, D.C., was led by:
   a)   Louis Farrakhan
   b)   David Koresh
   c)   H. Ross Perot
   d)   Rush Limbaugh

14. Oklahoma City made headlines in 1995 as the site where:
   a)   FBI agents and federal marshals laid seige to the cabin of an armed white separatist
   b)   two high school students went on a shooting spree, killing thirteen
   c)   federal agents battled members of a religious sect called the Branch Davidians
   d)   a right-wing extremist bombed a federal office building, killing 168 people

15. In early 1999, the Senate convicted President Clinton of:
   a)   perjury
   b)   obstruction of justice
   c)   perjury and obstruction of justice
   d)   neither perjury nor obstruction of justice

True or False

1. President Bush responded to the Chinese crackdown on dissidents in Tiananmen Square by breaking off relations with Beijing.

2. During the Gulf War, President Bush persuaded both Egypt and Israel to join the coalition opposing Iraq.

3. Cutbacks in defense spending following the end of the Cold War contributed to a U.S. recession in the early 1990s.

4. The 1992 Los Angeles riot erupted after a jury acquitted four policeman of assaulting an unarmed black man.

5. In 1992, Patrick Buchanan captured the largest fraction of the presidential vote ever won by a third-party candidate.

6. In 1996, Congress passed a sweeping welfare reform act over President Clinton's veto.

7. Terrorists linked to Osama bin Laden attacked the *Exxon Valdez* while it was anchored in Yemen.

8. The prosperity of the 1990s was largely due to technological innovations which increased worker productivity.

9. The Internet was originally conceived in the late 1960s as a network that would preserve communications in the event of a nuclear attack.

10. By the late 1990s, most Americans agreed that the large number of immigrants to the United States made bilingual education necessary.

11. The national crime rate declined in the 1990s.

12. At the end of the 1990s, half of all Americans exercised regularly.

13. The United States achieved a balanced federal budget in 1999.

14. The Supreme Court ruled that tobacco was an addictive drug, subject to regulation by the Food and Drug Administration.

15. Bill Clinton was the first American president to be impeached.

SOURCES FOR FURTHER RESEARCH

Books

Peter Baker, *The Breach: Inside the Impeachment and Trial of William Jefferson Clinton* (2000).

Michael Beschloss and Strobe Talbott, *At the Highest Levels: The Inside Story of the End of the Cold War* (1993).

James MacGregor Burns and Georgia J. Sorenson, *Dead Center: Clinton-Gore Leadership and the Perils of Moderation* (1999).

Colin Campbell and Bert A. Rockman, eds., *The Clinton Presidency: First Appraisals* (1996).

Kevin Davies, *Cracking the Genome: Inside the Race to Unlock Human DNA* (2001).

Elizabeth Drew, *On the Edge: The Clinton Presidency* (1994).

———, *Showdown: The Struggle Between the Gingrich Congress and the Clinton White House* (1996).

Nelson George, *Hip Hop America* (1998).

John Robert Greene, *The Presidency of George Bush* (2000).

Katie Hafner and Matthew Lyon, *Where Wizards Stay Up Late: The Origins of the Internet* (1996).

Michael Hogan, ed., *The End of the Cold War: Its Meaning and Implications* (1992).

Steven Hurst, *The Foreign Policy of the Bush Administration: In Search of a New World Order* (1999).

Daniel Ichbiah and Susan L. Knepper, *The Making of Microsoft: How Bill Gates and His Team Created the World's Most Successful Software Company* (1991).

Michael Lewis, *The New New Thing: A Silicon Valley Story* (2000).

David Maraniss, *First in His Class: A Biography of Bill Clinton* (1995).

David Mervin, *George Bush and the Guardianship Presidency* (1996).

Richard A. Posner, *An Affair of State: The Investigation, Impeachment, and Trial of President Clinton* (1999).

Stanley Renshon, *High Hopes: The Clinton Presidency and the Politics of Ambition* (1996).

Steven Schier, ed., *The Postmodern Presidency: Bill Clinton's Legacy in U.S. Politics* (2000).

David Shipler, *A Country of Strangers: Blacks and Whites in America* (1997).

Micah L. Sifry and Christopher Cerf, eds., *The Gulf War Reader: History, Documents, Opinions* (1991).

Catherine McNicol Stock, *Rural Radicals: Righteous Rage in the American Grain* (1996).

Roberto Suro, *Strangers Among Us: How Latino Immigration Is Transforming America* (1998).

Jeffrey Toobin, *A Vast Conspiracy: The Real Story of the Sex Scandal That Nearly Brought Down a President* (1999).

Nicholas Wade, *Life Script: How the Human Genome Discoveries Will Transform Medicine and Enhance Your Health* (2001).

James Wallace and Jim Erickson, *Hard Drive: Bill Gates and the Making of Microsoft* (1992).

James Wallace, *Overdrive: Bill Gates and the Race to Control Cyberspace* (1997).

Alan Wolfe, *One Nation, After All: What Middle-Class Americans Really Think About* (1998).

Bob Woodward, *The Commanders* (1991).

———, *The Agenda: Inside the Clinton White House* (1994).

Videos

Cold War (20 hours, PBS Video, 1998). This twenty-four-part documentary, originally produced for CNN, uses newly released footage to tell the story of the Cold

War. Episode 23, "The Wall Comes Down: 1989," traces the breakup of the Soviet bloc and shows East and West Germans tearing down the Berlin Wall. Episode 24, "Conclusions: 1989–1991," explores the issues that ultimately led to the dissolution of the Soviet Union and the peaceful end of the Cold War.

The Gulf War (120 minutes, PBS Home Video, 1996). Originally produced for PBS's *Frontline* program, this documentary highlights the backstage struggle between American political leaders and the American military and between the generals themselves.

Clarence Thomas and Anita Hill: Public Hearing, Private Pain (58 minutes, PBS Video, 1992). This program, originally shown on PBS's *Frontline,* discusses the confirmation hearings of Supreme Court justice Clarence Thomas, including the charges of sexual harrassment by Anita Hill and the reactions of African Americans.

The War Room (96 minutes, Vidmark Entertainment, 1994). This riveting documentary follows the Clinton presidential campaign from the New Hampshire primary to the victory party ten months later. At the center are the two men most responsible for Clinton's victory: James Carville, the campaign manager, and George Stephanopoulos, the communications director.

The Clinton Years (120 minutes, PBS Video, 2001). Drawing on interviews with key members of the Clinton administration, this *Frontline* program examines Bill Clinton's eight years in office.

Yugoslavia: Death of a Nation (250 minutes, Discovery Channel, 1995). Using interviews with principal figures and archival footage, this five-part program examines the bloody war in the former Yugoslavia. It begins with the country's initial breakup following Tito's death and the loss of Communist control and concludes with the Dayton peace plan in the fall of 1995.

Nerds 2.0.1: A Brief History of the Internet (180 minutes, PBS Home Video and Warner Home Video [distributor], 1998). This three-part series examines the ins and outs of one of the nation's most volatile industries: the Internet. The first episode, "Networking the Nerds," examines how the seeds of the Internet were planted by Sputnik and shows how it grew out of Cold War competition with the Soviet Union. The second episode, "Serving the Suits," discusses the advent of the personal computer and the drive to connect PCs to a network. The final episode, "Wiring the World," focuses on the development of the World Wide Web and the browsers that made using it a friendly experience for many.

Rhetorical Highlights from the Impeachment of Bill Clinton (105 minutes, Educational Video Group, 2000). This documentary traces the legislative impeachment of Bill Clinton. It includes the questioning of witnesses, the debate over the impeachment process in the House, the Senate trial, and the final vote tally.

Web Resources

The George Bush Presidential Library and Museum reproduces scores of Bush's speeches and other public papers in a format that can either be browsed by date or searched by keyword. The library also offers biographies of George and Barbara Bush, as well as photos of the Bush family, George Bush's activities during the Gulf War, state visits and economic summits, and selected commemorations and signing ceremonies.

http://bushlibrary.tamu.edu/home.html

The Smithsonian Institution's National Museum of American History offers "The Disability Rights Movement," a virtual exhibit examining the history of activism by those who have fought for the civil rights of people with disabilities. The website, established to commemorate the tenth anniversary of the Americans with Disabilities Act, reproduces the interactive kiosk that accompanies the museum's physical exhibition.

http://americanhistory.si.edu/ve/index.htm

"The Gulf War," a companion site to the PBS *Frontline* special of the same name, presents oral histories by Washington decision makers, battlefield commanders, Iraqi officials, and analysts. Those interviewed include General Colin Powell, Defense Secretary Dick Cheney, Soviet leader Mikhail Gorbachev, and General Norman Schwarzkopf. The site also offers the war stories of selected pilots and soldiers, a chronology of the war, various maps, and information on weapons and other technologies used in Desert Storm.

http://www.pbs.org/wgbh/pages/frontline/gulf/

A wealth of material on the collapse of Communism in Central and Eastern Europe and the dissolution of the Soviet Union can be found at "Cold War," the award-winning website set up by CNN to accompany its 1998 series by the same name. Visitors may read excerpts from Gorbachev's 1988 speech to the United Nations, in which he announced drastic cuts in the Soviet military presence in Eastern Europe; view CNN footage and slide shows illustrating the fall of various Communist regimes; and listen to audio clips of interviews with George Bush, Mikhail Gorbachev, and the Hungarian prime minister. The site also offers CNN's coverage of the 1991 coup attempt against Gorbachev, as well as the text of Boris Yeltsin's speech denouncing the coup.

http://www.cnn.com/SPECIALS/cold.war/

The Internet Public Library's "Presidents of the United States Site (POTUS)" offers extensive material on each of the nation's forty-three presidents. The portions of the site dedicated to George Herbert Walker Bush and William Jefferson Clinton contain election results for the 1988, 1992 and 1996 presidential elections, a list of each president's cabinet members, a personal fact sheet on each president, links to other political figures and presidents, material on First Ladies Barbara

Bush and Hillary Rodham Clinton, a sound and image file, primary sources, and links to other related sites.

http://www.ipl.org/ref/POTUS/

The Clinton Presidential Center website provides a biography of the nation's forty-second president and a time line highlighting the legislative accomplishments of his administration. A "Legacies" section contains personal recollections submitted by various Americans, as well as citizens' letters to the president. The website, like the Clinton Presidential Library, is still under construction, but it will eventually offer hundreds of documents and photographs associated with the Clinton presidency.

http://www.clintonpresidentialcenter.com/

A State of Shock: 2000–2001

CHAPTER OUTLINE

I. Election 2000
   A. The Campaign
      1) Major-party candidates
         a) Gore and Lieberman
         b) Bush and Cheney
      2) Strategies and platforms
         a) Gore: ambivalence toward Clinton
         b) Bush: "compassionate conservatism"
      3) Third-party candidates
         a) Patrick Buchanan
         b) Ralph Nader
   B. Disputed Outcome
      1) Florida: the pivotal state
      2) Charges of voting irregularities
      3) Court rulings
         a) Florida State Supreme Court
         b) U.S. Supreme Court
      4) Popular outrage
         a) criticism of the Supreme Court
         b) criticism of the electoral college
         c) disparities in quality of vote-counting machines
      5) Analysis of the vote
II. The Bush Presidency: Beginnings
   A. Early Steps
      1) Conciliatory tone
      2) Cabinet appointments
   B. Governing from the Right

           1) Conservative domestic agenda
           2) Signs of recession
           3) Tax cut
    C. Resistance and Jeffords
           1) Energy and the environmental policies
           2) Growing popular and congressional resistance
           3) Jeffords's defection from Republican Party
           4) Congressional standoff
    D. America First
           1) Bush's isolationist tendencies
           2) National Missile Defense
           3) Global warming
               a) rejection of the Kyoto Protocol
               b) European reaction
III. Struck by Terror
    A. September 11, 2001
    B. Bush Takes Charge
           1) Immediate steps
           2) Launching a "war on terror"
           3) Securing the home front
           4) Building an international coalition
           5) Public reactions
           6) The war in Afghanistan
    C. State of the Nation
           1) Patriotism and globalism
           2) A sense of vulnerability
           3) Sources of Muslim anti-Americanism
               a) U.S. support for Israel
               b) United States' vanguard role in globalization
           4) Disbelief and vulnerability
           5) Anthrax scare
           6) America is an idea
               a) worsening recession
               b) expanded power for law enforcement
               c) rights, liberties, and the American idea

SOURCES FOR FURTHER RESEARCH

Books

Peter L. Bergen, *Holy War, Inc.: Inside the Secret World of Osama bin Laden* (2001).
Yossef Bodansky, *Bin Laden: The Man Who Declared War on America* (2001).

Alan M. Dershowitz, *Supreme Injustice: How the High Court Hijacked Election 2000* (2001).

Abner Greene, *Understanding the 2000 Election: A Guide to the Legal Battles that Decided the Presidency* (2001).

Mark Huband, *Warriors of the Prophet: The Struggle for Islam* (1998).

New York, September 11 by Magnum Photographers, introduced by David Halberstam (2001).

One Nation: America Remembers September 11, 2001 (2001).

Richard A. Posner, *Breaking the Deadlock: The 2000 Election, the Constitution, and the Courts* (2001).

Roger Simon, *Divided We Stand: How Al Gore Beat George Bush and Lost the Presidency* (2001).

Jeffrey Toobin, *Too Close to Call: The Thirty-Six Day Battle to Decide the 2000 Election* (2001).

Videos

George W. Bush: Election and Inauguration (86 minutes, MPI Home Video, 2001). This program, hosted by Dan Rather, examines the contested presidential election of 2000. It includes election night, the ensuing legal battles and recounts, street protests, the Supreme Court ruling, and George W. Bush's inaugural address.

Hunting Bin Laden (55 minutes, PBS Home Video, 2001). This documentary, originally broadcast as a *Frontline* segment, investigates Osama bin Laden, his followers, and the bombings of two African embassies in 1998. This version has been updated to include the September 11, 2001, attack on the World Trade Center.

Looking for Answers (60 minutes, PBS Home Video, 2001). This *Frontline* documentary discusses the September 11 terrorist attacks on the United States, the roots of hatred found in Egypt and Saudi Arabia, radical Islam, and the failure of U.S. intelligence that made the World Trade Center and Pentagon attacks possible.

Web Resources

The Internet Public Library's "Presidents of the United States Site (POTUS)" offers extensive material on each of the nation's forty-three presidents. The portion of the site dedicated to George Walker Bush contains election results for the 2000 presidential election, a list of Bush's cabinet members, a personal fact sheet on the president, links to other political figures and presidents, material on First Lady Laura Bush, a sound and image file, primary sources, and links to other related sites.

http://www.ipl.org/ref/POTUS/gwbush.html

"Research and Reference Resources: Events of September 11th" provides links to newspaper and magazine articles and audio and video clips related to the attacks on the World Trade Center and Pentagon, the anthrax scare, and terrorism issues more generally. The site, compiled by Gary Price, also offers connections to congressional hearings, CIA reports, Department of Defense news briefings, and other relevant documents produced by the United States and other governments.

http://www.freepint.com/gary/91101.html

ANSWERS

CHAPTER 17

Multiple Choice

1. b
2. d
3. d
4. c
5. a
6. d
7. d
8. b
9. d
10. b
11. c
12. b
13. d
14. a
15. b

True or False

1. T
2. F
3. T
4. F
5. F
6. F
7. T
8. F
9. T
10. T
11. F
12. T
13. F
14. T
15. F

CHAPTER 18

Multiple Choice

1. c
2. d
3. d
4. b
5. d
6. c
7. b
8. d
9. d
10. a
11. d
12. c
13. c
14. a
15. c

True or False

1. T
2. F
3. F
4. T
5. F
6. T
7. F
8. F
9. T
10. F
11. F
12. T
13. T
14. F
15. F

CHAPTER 19

Multiple Choice

1. d
2. b
3. b
4. a
5. d
6. a

7. b
8. b
9. d
10. d
11. b
12. c
13. c
14. c
15. b

True or False

1. F
2. T
3. F
4. F
5. T
6. F
7. T
8. F
9. T
10. T
11. F
12. F
13. T
14. F
15. T

CHAPTER 20

Multiple Choice

1. a
2. d
3. b
4. d
5. c
6. b
7. a
8. c
9. d
10. c
11. d
12. b

13. b
14. c
15. d

True or False

1. F
2. T
3. F
4. F
5. T
6. F
7. F
8. F
9. T
10. T
11. F
12. F
13. T
14. T
15. T

CHAPTER 21

Multiple Choice

1. b
2. d
3. c
4. c
5. d
6. c
7. d
8. c
9. d
10. b
11. d
12. a
13. c
14. b
15. d

True or False

1. F
2. T
3. F
4. F
5. T
6. F
7. T
8. T
9. F
10. T
11. T
12. F
13. F
14. F
15. T

CHAPTER 22

Multiple Choice

1. a
2. b
3. c
4. a
5. b
6. c
7. d
8. b
9. c
10. b
11. c
12. c
13. d
14. b
15. d

True or False

1. T
2. T
3. F
4. F
5. F
6. T

7. T
8. T
9. F
10. F
11. T
12. T
13. F
14. T
15. T

CHAPTER 23

Multiple Choice

1. b
2. d
3. d
4. d
5. b
6. d
7. d
8. a
9. d
10. b
11. a
12. c
13. a
14. c
15. b

True or False

1. F
2. T
3. T
4. F
5. F
6. F
7. T
8. F
9. F
10. T
11. F
12. F

13. T
14. F
15. F

CHAPTER 24

Multiple Choice

1. a
2. c
3. c
4. a
5. c
6. d
7. a
8. d
9. d
10. b
11. c
12. d
13. c
14. b
15. a

True or False

1. F
2. T
3. F
4. T
5. T
6. T
7. T
8. F
9. T
10. T
11. F
12. F
13. T
14. F
15. F

CHAPTER 25

Multiple Choice

1. a
2. b
3. a
4. b
5. c
6. d
7. a
8. b
9. b
10. d
11. a
12. a
13. d
14. d
15. c

True or False

1. F
2. T
3. F
4. T
5. F
6. F
7. F
8. T
9. F
10. T
11. T
12. T
13. F
14. F
15. F

CHAPTER 26

Multiple Choice

1. b
2. c
3. d
4. c

5. c
6. b
7. a
8. a
9. d
10. b
11. c
12. a
13. c
14. d
15. b

True or False

1. F
2. T
3. F
4. F
5. T
6. T
7. F
8. F
9. F
10. F
11. F
12. F
13. F
14. T
15. T

CHAPTER 27

Multiple Choice

1. b
2. c
3. d
4. c
5. d
6. c
7. b
8. a
9. c
10. a

11. c
12. d
13. d
14. c
15. b

True or False

1. F
2. T
3. T
4. T
5. T
6. F
7. F
8. F
9. T
10. F
11. T
12. F
13. T
14. F
15. T

CHAPTER 28

Multiple Choice

1. b
2. b
3. d
4. c
5. a
6. b
7. a
8. a
9. b
10. b
11. c
12. c
13. c
14. d
15. c

True or False

1. F
2. T
3. F
4. T
5. T
6. T
7. T
8. F
9. T
10. F
11. F
12. F
13. F
14. F
15. T

CHAPTER 29

Multiple Choice

1. d
2. a
3. b
4. c
5. c
6. b
7. d
8. d
9. a
10. a
11. c
12. a
13. d
14. d
15. c

True or False

1. F
2. T
3. F
4. T

5. F
6. F
7. T
8. T
9. T
10. T
11. F
12. T
13. T
14. T
15. F

CHAPTER 30

Multiple Choice

1. b
2. d
3. a
4. b
5. c
6. a
7. b
8. c
9. b
10. a
11. d
12. d
13. b
14. b
15. d

True or False

1. F
2. T
3. T
4. F
5. F
6. T
7. T
8. F
9. T
10. F

11. T
12. F
13. F
14. T
15. F

CHAPTER 31

Multiple Choice

1. b
2. b
3. a
4. b
5. a
6. c
7. d
8. b
9. b
10. d
11. d
12. b
13. d
14. b
15. d

True or False

1. T
2. T
3. T
4. F
5. F
6. F
7. F
8. T
9. T
10. T
11. F
12. T
13. F
14. F
15. T

CHAPTER 32

Multiple Choice

1. b
2. d
3. a
4. c
5. a
6. d
7. b
8. d
9. d
10. c
11. d
12. d
13. b
14. c
15. c

True or False

1. T
2. T
3. F
4. F
5. F
6. T
7. T
8. F
9. T
10. T
11. F
12. T
13. F
14. T
15. F

CHAPTER 33

Multiple Choice

1. c
2. d

3. a
4. a
5. d
6. b
7. d
8. b
9. b
10. a
11. d
12. d
13. a

14. d
15. d

True or False

1. F
2. F
3. T
4. T
5. F
6. F

7. F
8. T
9. T
10. F
11. T
12. T
13. T
14. F
15. F